Becoming
a happy family

PATHWAYS TO THE FAMILY SOUL

Additional Books by Susan Smith Kuczmarski

The Sacred Flight of the Teenager: A Parent's Guide to Stepping Back and Letting Go

The Family Bond: Inspiring Tips for Creating a Closer Family

Apples Are Square: Thinking Differently About Leadership (co-authored with Thomas D. Kuczmarski)

Values-Based Leadership (co-authored with Thomas D. Kuczmarski)

Becoming a happy family

PATHWAYS TO THE FAMILY SOUL

Susan Smith Kuczmarski, Ed.D.

BOOK ENDS
PUBLISHING

Book Ends Publishing
Chicago, IL

Publisher: Book Ends Publishing
Cover design by Christophe Bardot/Tanen Directed Advertising
Page design by Caron Dickinson/Tanen Directed Advertising
Interior illustrations by Marci Jarog

Printed in the United States of America

This book is dedicated to my awesome mother, Bula Smith, who lived to be 100 years old. If crosswords, Jeopardy, chocolate, enjoying a great laugh and helping others have anything to do with this longevity, let's all follow her lead.

CONTENTS

About the Author

Susan Smith Kuczmarski, Ed.D. has the pulse on today's families. Trained as a cultural anthropologist, she has extensively researched how children learn social skills and how adolescents become leaders. Her teaching reflects her passion for serving others, knowing self, finding common ground, letting creativity reign and rooting for others.

She currently teaches leadership courses to educators and executives at Northwestern University's Kellogg School of Management and entrepreneurship to pre-collegiate teens at Loyola University Chicago. During the course of a career that spans more than three decades, she has taught at eight universities, worked in three nonprofit educational organizations, including the United Nations, and co-founded an innovation consulting firm, Kuczmarski Innovation, in Chicago.

She is the author of four award-winning books, two on parenting and two on leadership. *The Sacred Flight of the Teenager: A Parent's Guide to Stepping Back and Letting Go* (Book Ends Publishing, 2003) received the prestigious "Seal of Approval" award from the National Parenting Center and a "Book of the Year Award" from *ForeWord Magazine*. In 2012, Deepak Chopra wrote the foreword to the Second Edition of *Apples Are Square: Thinking Differently About Leadership* (Kaplan Publishing, 2007). It received the coveted "2007 Best Business Book Award" from *Fast Company Magazine* and has been printed in multiple languages, with editions in China, Taiwan and Korea. The book champions six innovative leadership qualities—humility, transparency, compassion, inclusiveness, collaboration and values-based decisiveness. To encourage family relationship building, she wrote *The Family Bond: Inspiring Tips for Creating a Closer Family* (McGraw-Hill, 2000). It is a right-brain guide to creating a family atmosphere in which love can thrive. Her first book, *Values-Based Leadership* (Prentice Hall, 1995), pioneered the expression of personal values in the workplace.

Dr. Kuczmarski speaks to parents, leaders and educators. She holds a Doctorate in Education and two master's degrees from Columbia University in New York City, where she was named an International Fellow, and an undergraduate degree from Colorado College, where she has returned to teach leadership. Dr. Kuczmarski is a regular radio and television guest, devoted to issues of the contemporary family. She has appeared on the *Today Show,* is widely quoted in print across the country, and has been listed in *Who's Who in the World* for 12 years. Her speeches, seminars, research, teaching and consulting have made her a leading expert on family bonding, teens, leadership and energizing teams. She currently serves as the chairman of the trustees of the Chicago City Day School.

Susan lives in Chicago with her husband and partner in life, Tom Kuczmarski. They have three adult sons. Visit her website at: www.sacredflight.com.

About the Illustrator

Marci Jarog is a management consul-
tant and editor living in Lakeview, Chicago, with
her husband, Jon, and growing young family.

She graduated with honors from the University of Chicago with a degree in Philosophy and
holds a Masters in Journalism from Northwestern University's Medill School of Journalism.
She has written extensively for *Bloomberg News*
and leads innovation projects for multi-billion dollar brands in the U.S. and
internationally.

Jarog grew up on a cattle ranch in Oklahoma and credits the open prai-
rie for instilling the patience, grit and creativity she's relied on as a writer,
editor, classical violinist and Ironman triathlete.

Acknowledgements

I am especially grateful to Tom Kuczmarski, who offered guidance, support and innovative perspective at every bump and turn, then optimism to keep moving forward. Special thanks to Beth Ylvisaker, who lent her kind and generous ear and creative insight at many points in the lengthy writing process. Christina Van Pelt and Reven Fellars each read an earlier draft of the entire book, gave their valuable feedback and editorial comments, and helped move it to the next phase. To Galeta Kaar Clayton, a tireless and timeless role model for families, I extend my deepest respect and gratitude.

A high-spirited and indefatigable group of friends and colleagues invested considerable time into the research project, helping to carve out the emerging ideas. I listened deeply and attentively to their thoughts and concerns. Acknowledging their role and generous involvement, special gratitude is given to Barbara Smith-Bacon, Patty Brottman, Thomas Chalmers, Martha Donovan, Keira Doolittle, Lisa Dunn, Olivia Jee, Rosalyn King, Michele Miller, Sally Parsons, Colleen Ransdell, Erica Regunberg, Barbara Kay Richmond, Laurie Smith, Linda Tucker Smith, Luke Tanen and Chrissy Washburn.

Marci Jarog, the book's gifted editor, offered brilliant editorial and content suggestions and comments. Her impact was enormous, contributing to the book's overall flow and readability. Gratefully, I refer to Marci as "the boss." She played a vital role in the "birthing" process.

And finally, to all those individuals whose personal stories I shared. To them, it probably appears like I was not "writing" but only "dictating" and adding a dramatic flare. This "troop" includes my three adult sons, John Kuczmarski, James Kuczmarski and Thomas Kuczmarski, and my two brothers and sisters-in-law, Dean Smith, Paul Smith, JoAnn Smith and Mary Smith. I suspect they are happy that the book has been completed. For each of you, and all those acknowledged here, I am deeply grateful. We are family.

Introduction

Ten years ago, I was interviewed by a panel of four teenagers on a radio show in North Carolina called "Teen Life." At the time I was making publicity rounds, promoting my second family book, *The Sacred Flight of the Teenager: A Parent's Guide to Stepping Back and Letting Go*. An articulate fourteen-year-old boy asked me a difficult question that would stump me for years. Since I was given an audio tape of my radio interview, I have played it back, word-for-word, at least a dozen times: "Our lives are so busy—are there tips you can give us, being so busy, to help us sit down and connect, you know, and talk for the little time that we have?"

While I often get asked this question by parents, this was the first time a young teen expressed it. I replied: "Sometimes we can find these openings by turning downtime into bond time. When we're sitting together in a car, for example, it's downtime, and a great opportunity for bonding, talking and connecting, if we turn off the music!" But I was not satisfied with my answer. To me, this teen was searching for a "bigger picture" antidote to his and our hectic-paced lifestyle. In effect, he wanted to know how to create a happy family.

My one hundred-year-old mother summed this huge problem up quite succinctly, "Life is too crowded!" This teen was searching for more than one-off interactions, and a more permanent way to feel connected with his family. Bonding as we sit together in a car isn't a deep-down systemic solution, even if the music is turned down! Instead,

> **"Our lives are so busy—are there tips you can give us, being so busy, to help us sit down and connect, you know, and talk for the little time that we have?"**

a bigger shift or "reset" is in order. Families are looking for ways to experience happiness, become aware of their family soul and better understand how to access, strengthen and nurture it.

Just as many writers devise ways to "enter" a creative, inspired, or sacred place—families too can seek out a happier, more soulful space. Could it possibly be found within the chaos of everyday family life? I believe it can. My goal in writing this book is to find simple ways for family members to identify and then care for their family soul. There is a higher, deeper and closer place within the life of the family that might be called the soul. I do not mean "soul" in the theological sense—one that potentially serves life after death. Rather, I mean a more real-world experience of soul that is connected to the ordinary, routine and everyday family scene. It is part of the day-to-day craft of building a close bond, and nurturing creative and caring individuals within it.

We may not always be aware of our desire—even longing—for the soulful in daily family life. We all live our lives in a family, but we often fail to use the essence and beauty of this togetherness to capture and experience the spirit within each of us, our dreams, our highest sense of self, and our connection to what I would call the "spirit of us." Caring for the soul of the family offers just this focus. It involves pushing out the family boundary to welcome and accept an amalgam of friends, family members, pets and special people from all sorts of circles—often creating new families in the process. Additionally, in researching the elusive topic of the soul, from my observations and from the observations of others captured in my interviews, I have unearthed six key experiences—humor, emotion, acceptance, renewal, togetherness and struggle. Each acts as a magnetic force that connects and strengthens our relationships to create a bond we call "family."

Two earlier drafts of this book can be found on my computer desktop. I am hesitant to share how many years I have been working on it. Let's just say the timing wasn't right! Not until I got out of my head and into the world—talking intimately with single and married people, parents and grandparents, twenty and early thirty something young adults and a variety of unique others—did I see the light! Trained as a cultural anthropologist, in-depth interviewing is what I do to understand and explain. The insights that surfaced in these interviews merged with my thoughts, confirming some and altering others, ultimately guiding me to this last version of the book, a rebirth.

I am grateful to the twenty-five individuals who poured out their hearts and souls for my effort. I know for a fact that each spent immense amounts of time, sometimes weeks, pondering my fifteen questions. (The interview guide is appended for those interested.) The material transcribed from the interviews became the "data" to guide my quest. All interviewees remain completely anonymous.

Becoming A Happy Family: Pathways to the Family Soul offers perspective, practices and paradigms to deepen and transform family life and care for the soul within it.

PART 1

Finding the Soul of the Family

1. Seek Happiness

"Someday after we have mastered the winds, the waves, the tides and gravity, we shall harness for the Divine the energies of the power of love. And then for the second time in the history of the world we will have discovered fire."

—Teillard de Chardin

Family bonds may last a lifetime, but family happiness can be elusive. We all share a search to find meaningful relationships. The institution of family can seem perfectly set up to provide the love and permanence that so nourishes our hearts.

And yet family can sometimes let us down. Some families lack a loving connection, some are a source of negative energy and some simply run off course amid the daily chaos and complexity of modern life.

> **The power to forge family relationships is within our grasp—not necessarily traditional family connections, but, like a kaleidoscope, a constellation of friendships and filial connections that create a living universe greater than the sum of its parts. This is what I call the "family soul."**

Despite these challenges, the power to forge family relationships is within our grasp—not necessarily traditional family connections, but, like a kaleidoscope, a constellation of friendships and filial connections that create a living universe greater than the sum of its parts. This is what I call the "family soul." It is among the greatest of human pursuits.

Family soul is the memories and traits that make the family unique, including rituals, stories, experiences, conflicts and love. It is the family's complex network of relationships, values and activities. It is how we talk, feel and interact when we're together. When family members discover and appreciate the unique individuality and relationships that exist within their family, a deep family connection can grow. They can become a happy family.

Family Happy Hour

The caretaker for the soul of our family was my mother. Let me share our last experience together, our final family "happy hour." Five of us—my two brothers, my sister-in-law, my oldest nephew and I—gathered in my ailing one hundred-year-old mom's small room to keep a watchful eye on her. I had spent the night in a cot in her room. The hospice staff that took care of her believed she was declining significantly and that the end was imminent. Since it was my sister-in-law's birthday, we had picked up a festive carrot cake with vanilla frosting to enjoy in my mom's presence. (By my conservative calculation she had made over eighteen hundred birthday cakes for family and friends in her long life.)

After we had finished our piece of cake, my brother asked my mom if she wanted a taste of the frosting. She nodded her head gently but eagerly. He put a tiny bit on her lips, following it with some ice-cold water on a stick sponge. She was delighted. Smiling sweetly, she softly said "That tastes good!" and one second later, gasped her last breath. We all held her tight, I squeezed her arm and you could feel her pulse decrease, become faint and then disappear. Then after a long forty-five seconds, she came back for a second last breath—this one much quieter but still graceful, like her life had been, and then no more pulse. Strong, generous, selfless and regal, she had touched many people during her long life.

It was *precisely* 5:00 pm when she passed away. I believe she had waited the entire day for this hour. I share this exact time of day with you because it was significant for our family. At five o'clock we *always* gathered together in our home. For as long as I can remember, from small child to grown adult, my dad elatedly opened the squeaky back door and walked in, marking the end of his work day. We could count on him, like ducks traveling south for the winter. There were drinks (he'd play the bartender) and snacks and it was a time to come together and experience family happiness.

But more, on this same day when my mom died, it turns out, precisely fifteen years earlier, my dad had passed away (well, minus 7 hours). Close enough. The moment in time was highly unusual and deserved reflection for this reason. Now a decade and a half later, I think there was the good chance that mom was meeting him for a long-awaited five o'clock "happy hour." Together again.

Mom and Dad as newlyweds on honeymoon in 1940.

The Family Kaleidoscope

Families have the opportunity to become a brightly lit, colorful kaleidoscope. As we look through the eyepiece, and give it a twirl, we can *see* that every word, smile and tear comes together to reveal a distinctive form and pattern to the family "picture." A caring environment helps each person mature and grow, become whole and learn love. Allies—family members and friends—support each other and teach us how to give and receive love. Gentleness, patience and kindness serve as our guides. Forcefulness, intolerance and excessive control can rob us of our sparkle. Most astonishingly, we can observe and feel a sense of connection, love, community support and security in the present. Hold each other a little closer, reach out a little farther and grasp the enormity of the impact of each heart connection. When you do, turn the kaleidoscope again, and

Families have the opportunity to become a brightly lit, colorful kaleidoscope. As we look through the eyepiece, and give it a twirl, we can see that every word, smile and tear comes together to reveal a distinctive form and pattern to the family "picture."

you will have experienced the soul of the family in motion, the happiest of sights.

Piecing Together the Family Puzzle

Every family wants to be happy. Let's explore and observe your family picture. Take out your kaleidoscope and look through the lens. *View* each of the "frames" (below) as discoveries, each one having surfaced from my research. I offer them to you here as guidelines in piecing together your family puzzle. We all lead busy lives. I want you to have these unearthed "findings" close at hand as you maneuver along the path to find the soul of your family. Each "frame" is integral to carving out a happy and dynamic family.

- *Recognize the three general roles that families might fulfill—functional, emotional and soulful.* If families are able to build a bridge to the soulful dimension, their energy, bond and connection can shift to a deeper, happier realm.

- *Acknowledge that each family has a soul.* It is the unspoken bond that is the origin of trust and faith and the reservoir of love and energy that unites the group. The tenor and tone of the family soul changes, as it does with life's events, challenges and situations.

- *Embrace how your family is unique.* Today's family is a broad and deep network of interconnections and relationships. Paralleling this refreshing diversity in membership and structure is the continual metamorphosis of one's sense of family.

- *Applaud the caretaker.* The caretaker is the champion for the soul of the family. Essential to the family flow and cohesion, caretakers accomplish several crucial tasks: they reach out to others and bring them closer, manage the various needs of each member, share what is going on in each other's lives, organize traditions and gatherings, and juggle conflict and change.

Through the Family Kaledioscope.

- ***Start a family of one's own.*** Twenty and thirty year olds are often-times transitioning between two families—the "old" birth family and a new-to-the-world family, created and launched through new relationship building. The family soul acts like sticky glue, connecting them to both.

- ***Welcome in-laws and special people into your fold.*** Inclusiveness can be infectious. Removing family hierarchies allows members to participate and share of themselves more freely. All family members are equal and this includes in-laws and others invited into the family network of relationships. Some may find this "welcoming" a difficult pill to swallow but the reward is worth the effort.

- *Bond with multiple friends.* Friends ignite and expand the spirit and energy of the family soul. They are integral to each member's inner learning, growth and happiness. So invite, include and involve others in your family scene, and treat them as family members. Friends enrich a family immeasurably.

- *Discover a soul friend.* Soul friends are deeply dedicated, exceptional friends with whom we share a very close bond. They can heal our hearts, reconnect us and fortify our energy to continue undeterred on our journey. Often acting as teachers, they inspire our personal learning and growth. They may give sage advice, an experienced ear or simply a fresh perspective, idea, or solution. Holding off evaluation or judgment, they serve as a sounding board, or road map, to help us along a difficult family path.

- *Add pets to the scene.* A deep, loving relationship with a family pet plays an enormous role in shaping the soul of a family. Pets help us get closer and they hold us together. We learn from our pets both how to love and how to accept love. Who would think a wagging tail would teach us some of the most essential lessons about communication, connection and unconditional love!

Family soul is the memories and traits that make the family unique, including rituals, stories, experiences, conflicts and love. It is the family's complex network of relationships, values and activities. It is how we talk, feel and interact when we're together. Explore and discover the distinctive patterns that are unique to your family picture.

2. Recognize the Roles of Family— Functional, Emotional and Soulful

A family protects us from the noise of the outer world. It provides a sanctuary where we can withdraw into silence and be alone, if we choose. We can forget everyday concerns and demands and just relax and open up to pure wonderment and joy. It can be a place where we discover a loving, tender and generous heart. Through our connections to one another – our togetherness – we are able to receive deep, enduring warmth and love. Our individual inner flames are ignited, nourished and renewed so we can live life from the center.

It is here too where we may first discover and experience who we are and what we might become. It is where we learn to work with weakness, inadequacy, deficiency, inability and even failure. Flaws and insecurity are at the heart of the individual, as they point the way to learning and growth. Family can be a place where we grow individually and come together. It is where we return, time and again, after we have changed and gotten older to share our journey with one another. These experiences comprise the heart of the family soul.

Like the imaginative world of a young child, a close family is brilliantly simple, yet fascinatingly complex. If such a family dynamic is reached, a profound connectedness can occur among its members. The energy of deep love is

> **A family protects us from the noise of the outer world.**

able to permeate the group. An unfathomable caring and compassion extends to each family member, who in turn feels loved and valued in a way they may not experience in the outside world. This connectedness sparks a passion for sharing and giving. The formerly mundane familiar family structure becomes alive, creative and profoundly close. How does this transformation from everyday ritual into a living organism of being and becoming occur?

My research identified three general roles that the family might fulfill—functional, emotional and soulful. On a daily basis, most tend to operate in only the first or second dimension of functional and emotional interaction. We infrequently experience the third dimension of the soul, which is so strong and supportive that it bolsters individual members and converts the family into a life-changing group. In this dimension, families experience an energy and togetherness that brings a far deeper meaning to the everyday rhythms of life.

How does this transformation from everyday ritual into a living organism of being and becoming occur?

Functional Roles

The family's functional roles may consist of the daily chores and activities that a family regularly tends to. These interactions require working together to manage the tasks and tediums of day-to-day life. They include preparing meals (for some families eating dinner together is not an everyday occurrence, sadly), walking the dog, shopping for food and other goods, going to work and school, and planning and engaging in a household project together. You will recognize functional activities immediately. These experiences bind the family into a sustainable community.

Emotional Roles

Participation in this functional community brings family members into social interactions, which, in turn, give rise to emotional expression. In this second dimension family members express love to one another through collective interaction and involvement in each other's daily activities. Our shared experiences—through everyday exchanges and communications—amplify our emotional connections. Members may help one another during difficult life circumstances. Or their emotional bond might simply be expressed through a forthright loving gesture such as a hug or a subtle act of listening. Emotional communication and appreciation are ways that members can infuse living presence into the heart and soul of the family spirit.

With a constant stream of tasks and responsibilities tied to jobs, activities, school, housework and friends, many singles and working couples tell me they do not make it beyond the second dimension. Unmistakably, they "get stuck." Nowadays, if families are able to make it through the week with their unruly schedules and countless activities, and still find time for moments of emotional connection and expression, it is probably a good week!

One parent shared this frustration when asked to explain her approach and mindset: "I think it becomes very difficult to care for the soul of the family as children grow and become engaged in school as well as after-school activities like athletics. We get busy with life and don't feed the soul." She added: "Any time we can steal together helps to nourish it—a simple board game, a movie outing, even a car ride to the grocery can allow that time together to happen. Some of the 'care' comes at mealtime where, without distraction, our family seems to be able to get twenty minutes of family time."

> **"We get busy with life and don't feed the soul...any time we can steal together helps to nourish it—a simple board game, a movie outing, even a car ride to the grocery can allow that time together to happen."**

Soulful Roles

If families are able to build a bridge to the third dimension—the soulful dimension—their bond has the ability to shift to a deeper realm. Family connections can become stronger. Relationships between family members find the space and energy to become more intense, earnest and reflective. While this occurs at the emotional level as well, accessing the family soul can help members take it up a notch to profoundly care about each other, desire to help one another develop and expand, and look after each other in supportive ways. How is it different at the soulful level? They now begin to nurture not only each other but also the family itself as a living pulse providing energy and nutrition apart from the everyday functional and emotional interactions. These families experience a changed energy. Too, there is mystery within their shared experiences. In this third dimension, family members begin to experience the soul of the family.

One wise parent likened nurturing the soul of the family to gardening—and the soul to the soil. If you don't have healthy soil, and you don't care for the soil of your garden, nothing is going to flourish. It is not about the roots, although roots of course help; it is all about the soil when you talk about growing things. Soul is the ground beneath the roots. When you talk about a tree, you talk about the strength of the trunk and the branches and the roots underneath, but the soil is what makes it last. It is what matters.

Soulful Practices—A Preview

While family members may make up a household, a household does not necessarily make up a family. Whereas emotional and functional interactions create a household, they do not entirely a family make! It is our more intimate interactions, mindset and values that create a family soul. Soulful practices are crucial—and often missing from the family scene.

Family members interviewed for this book continually expressed their frustration with not having the time or ability to access the higher-level, deeply intimate dimension. How can we tap into the energy and mystery of the soulful, particularly if simply managing our functional and emotional

> **While family members may make up a household, a household does not necessarily make up a family.**

interactions can be themselves overwhelming? Are there practical ways to transform mundane, functional activities into soul interactions? How might presence of mind and the expression of family values elevate household and everyday tasks to the level of the soulful? Let's begin to answer these vitally important questions. It is my great hope that the tools and insights contained here will serve as a launchpad for families to cultivate sanctuaries within household life, strengthen their family soul and expand their happiness.

There are three general roles that families might fulfill—functional, emotional and soulful. If they are able to build a bridge to the soulful dimension, their energy, bond and connection can shift to a deeper, happier realm.

3. Acknowledge That Each Family Has A Soul

There is no perfect family. We are all works in progress. We are all in the throes of familyhood struggling to find happiness. We all want to enhance our own family's spirit and energy, deepen our connections and, just maybe, transform a wounded family soul into a healthy one, or a dormant family soul into an active one.

Every family experiences imbalance, some more than others. I hope you will walk away with a clear picture of how to better care for your family's soul and, just as importantly, how to engage and encourage other family members in this quest.

I hope you will walk away with a clear picture of how to better care for your family's soul and, just as importantly, how to engage and encourage other family members in this quest.

The Energy That Unites Us

You can't touch the soul of the family, but you are touched by it every day. We can think of the soul as the loving bonds or "sticky glue" that hold the family together without resistance or chafing. No two family souls are the same, just as no two individual souls are the same. The soul of the family is the spirit and energy source of its members. It is the overarching unbreakable bond that links us together. The elements of the soul are the core values that parents transfer to their children, and the respect and regard that parents have for each other that their children witness. A family can generate a healthy family soul that is optimistic, tolerant and loving.

Or it can generate a wounded family soul that is tentative, defensive and depleting.

The soul of the family can also serve as a moral compass for family members, the ground wire when we have lost our point of reference for understanding and interacting with the world around us. Our experience of family can guide how we operate in outside relationships with the larger world. We've all fallen down at some point, or have made compromised decisions that have taken us down a wrong path. The soul of the family can help to remind us who we are, where we come from and that we are not alone, like it or not. The soul of the family helps us to persevere through the worst times, to endure and, hopefully, to thrive.

> **A family can generate a healthy family soul that is optimistic, tolerant and loving. Or it can generate a wounded family soul that is tentative, defensive and depleting.**

The soul's work, then, is elastic and invisible, but vast and limitless. Just as the thread that connects us to all other living things, the soul of the family is that thread which runs through each individual and connects the family as a sacred unit.

> **The soul's work, then, is elastic and invisible, but vast and limitless. Just as the thread that connects us to all other living things, the soul of the family is that thread which runs through each individual and connects the family as a sacred unit.**

How the Family Soul Shifts and Evolves

The soul of the family changes and evolves through birth, life and death. These major events shape its tenor and tone, as do life's challenges and complexities. The family soul can be buoyed by good news. Or it can succumb to disintegration and despair with tragedy and misfortune.

In my family's case, the shoe remembers those who have gotten married! Let me explain. My dad had a pair of classy black men's shoes, the kind you wear when you dress up. My oldest brother, Dean, put them on for his son's wedding this year and they became the focus of his father-of-the-groom speech. Outlandish to even consider, these shoes are now seventy-four years old. They have been worn for eight different family weddings—four times: by my dad at his wedding (in 1940), at Dean's wedding (in 1971), at my wedding (in 1976), and at my brother Paul's wedding (in 1988), plus four times by Dean at his four adult children's weddings. These "historic" sparkling shiny and undeniably proud shoes might offer an explanation as to why we invent foolish and outrageous dance moves at family weddings, twirling and whirling, most certainly appearing unusual if not fanatical to others on the floor. These old shoes have been shaped by family weddings—and dance steps—as if the shoe passionately "remembers" those who have gotten married and danced into our lives.

The personality of each individual contributes to the overall chemistry of the family soul as parents (and friends) help meld new additions into the family network. As time passes individuals grow, mature and fulfill their dreams and potential. Their personalities take shape and they become fuller or more complete expressions of themselves. Love grows and the soul adjusts and modifies. Just look to the arrival of a newborn—nothing alights a family soul like a new addition! A new family member is a glorious one-of-a-kind experience. With each new person, (even in-laws!), the soul of the family grows.

In the opposite way, an addiction can rob a family of individuals and their qualities. Tragedy or personal challenge can halt the flow and progress of the shared journey, disrupt relationships and weaken the bond. A family must make adjustments, learn and reset its course.

One interviewed parent likened this changing process to breaking in a pair of new shoes. In the beginning the new shoes are stiff and uncomfortable, they squeak and they rub, but then as one wears them, they get broken in and eventually fit. As time goes by and as children grow and maturity sets in, along with the benefit of life experience and wisdom, family connections becomes more internalized. Now, not so "new," parents are less pressured to proactively nurture togetherness; it becomes ingrained, a bit like the old shoes. If members have a strong family connection, the essence of the family prevails across all borders. Even extending across generations, the soul of the family is imbued with those who are no longer living, who have been a special part of family members' lives. The shoes are shaped by every place the family has been together, as if the shape and feel of the shoe "remembers" those who have passed.

Experiencing Family Soul— What are the Signs?

How do you know if the family soul had been experienced? One interviewed twenty-something shared: "It is just like falling in love, it's a feeling. Relationships are deep-seated and integrated into 'who I am.' One is truly happy when spending time, laughing and just hanging out. When we leave, there is a void." The litmus test, said this young adult, who was departing after a weekend with her two sisters: "I oftentimes cry. That is how I know."

So how do you know if you are experiencing the soul of the family? The simple reply is: The shoe that was once new and stiff finally feels comfortable! While difficult to answer, one pragmatic parent said:

> **"When we leave, there is a void."**

"When you get up from the dinner table and you feel like all the family members have connected in some meaningful way. It doesn't have to be through deep conversation. In fact it can be a good laugh, or even a moment of agreement on an issue, big or small, that sparks the soul of the family." There is a pause amidst the chaos. You feel you have arrived somewhere real with your family, though transient; you have accessed a rare level of intimacy.

Another answer: you know you've experienced the soul of the family when you feel deep harmony with the ones you love. It is different from good times with friends in this sense. In fact, there is something extraordinary happening. One parent described it this way: "You feel oneness with each other, when your individual meaning and purpose in life flows throughout your family members in the form of happiness and harmony.

"In fact it can be a good laugh, or even a moment of agreement on an issue, big or small, that sparks the soul of the family." There is a pause amidst the chaos. You feel you have arrived somewhere real with your family, though transient; you have accessed a rare level of intimacy.

It's that easy comfortable feeling you have with the family, enhanced by those moments of pure joy or unbridled hilarity that are grounded in common intimacy. No one is on edge, no one feels judged. It's being in sync without having to analyze it. You feel you can handle life's triumphs and disappointments. You feel connected and uplifted."

Analogous to "music having soul," the rhythm is natural, has groove and flows to its own beat. You know you've experienced family soul because you feel like yourself while also connected with an organism beyond yourself.

This sense of "oneness" is not limited to biological family members. This feeling of experiencing the family soul or "flow" was persuasively shared by another interviewee. Her father's ashes were to be consecrated into their church's garden wall where her mother's were laid years prior. One hundred people crowded together in the sanctuary to witness this event at the memorial service. She shared: "As we stood there shoulder to shoulder in this little area and the blessing had finished, the minister said, 'We will now go into the sanctuary. Family members should go first. Where are the family

SOMETHING
IN THE
SOIL

members?' And I said, 'We are all the family members.' And we were. It didn't matter who went first or last."

Nurturing the Soul—How to?

Like soil, we nurture the family soul by caring for it and by focusing on its health. Advises one parent: "It is an inheritance and we are the stewards. It is not a tangible bequest, nor is it about genes; it is something that one receives that is passed down. We are the stewards of it. We live it, we model it, we don't teach it, we nurture it by example." The richer the soil is, the richer the taste of the fruit becomes. Strip the soil by over using it without replenishment and it will not only fail to produce, but will blow away as dust.

The family connection needs nurturing to thrive. But what do we do to enrich a family's soul? Quite simply, when family members talk, share, and recall memories, they add nutrients. The family soul is also cared for by attention, humor, listening, kindness, being together, doing things and even, as some parents noted, by writing, thinking and praying together as a family.

> **The richer the soil is, the richer the taste of the fruit becomes. Strip the soil by over using it without replenishment and it will not only fail to produce, but will blow away as dust.**

A family's soul has to be cultivated, just like one would nurture love and friendship. Focused as we all are on the small details of everyday life, it can be difficult to remember that the intimacy we share as a family—which is also grounds for conflicts—is what knits us together. Shared one parent, "As a family engaged and growing in and into our individual lives, we preserve a selection of casual dinners, holiday traditions and vacations with few external distractions. During these times, we share a variety of opinions and views without judgment (well, most of the time!) often over lengthy meals. And, on holidays, especially Christmas, we treasure silly traditions that make us feel secure, because they are familiar and they are 'ours.'" She adds, "In between we

> **"We treasure silly traditions that make us feel secure, because they are familiar and they are 'ours.' "**

try to ground ourselves with hugs, frequent communication and the more traditional verbal expression of our love for one another. I am a dedicated believer in hugs. There is nothing like the intimacy of touch to express affection or love. Even when we do push each other's buttons, the 'soul' helps us to recover from the hurt or insecurity that these jibes can cause. Apologies are acceptable and accepted."

The Mysteries That Define the Family Soul

If you listen to soul, or rock, or country music, it stimulates a wide range of emotions – it can be ecstatic, it can be sad. Think of the soul of the family in the same way. It keeps us all together when it's good. It gives us joy in being together. It also gives us a sense of security. Shared one parent: "For our children, there is a great sense of comfort in knowing that there is this Rock of Gibraltar kind of thing. We are not out to change. It is something that can be counted upon. There is this shared identity (who you are) and everyone is in sync with that."

While the family soul is too elusive to box into a strict definition, it has several enduring characteristics. It is not a perishable thing. It is not going to expire. There is no "best if used by" date on it. It has timelessness. Shared another parent: "Through it all, our family has endured. We respect and acknowledge that we can't make it alone, and that we need one another through the best of times, and the worst of times. We know that even though we can fall down, we can get back up again."

As the mystery of the family soul unfolds, it can enrich our lives in many ways: providing personal identity, clarity on individual and family values and the ability to give and receive love. Unearths one interviewed grandparent: "The family soul acknowledges and teaches who you are as a person and how to live and fulfill your life. It helps one persevere in hard circumstances, and celebrate the happy times. Everyone is equal and must get along. People love you and believe in you."

Perhaps the greatest mystery of the family soul is its ability to unite family members across ages, geographies and personalities. "My daughters and husband love spending time with my extended family. We have reunions every two years where all forty-one of us get together (we live in six different states all across the country). We do mini-geographical gatherings for the holidays and then we all do individual visits. We always play games, music, go sledding or skating. We just enjoy being in the moment and spending time and we can always count on each other when someone needs help, regardless of what it is. My daughters feel comfortable confiding in any of their aunts or cousins, and my husband loves jamming with all the brothers-in-law and all our kids who are all musically inclined." You get the picture here. The family soul is simply the experience of the *energy* that exudes when the family is together.

Every family has a soul. It is the unspoken bond that is the origin of trust and faith and the reservoir of love and energy that unites the group. The tenor and tone of the family soul changes, as it does with life's events, challenges and situations.

4. Embrace How Your Family Is Unique

Each of us has relationships that may constitute our sense of family. No two families are the same, just as no two individuals are the same. Relatives and friends, even our beloved pets, can contribute to the family soul. Families can become stronger and more connected if they not only recognize the soul that exists, what makes it unique, and how to care for it, but who the members are.

We are shaped by are our families and what we make of them. You can feel when you grow together, and you can feel when you grow apart. Though our need for family is innate, we possess the creativity and complexity as humans to draw our own unique definitions of what family is. Family can be a much broader network of relationships beyond those that are strictly biological. "Family" can include all the parents, siblings, friends, mentors and even pets whom we love and who love us back.

Your Family Composition and Story

Who is your family and how do you discover it? We have our relatives of course. But let's take away biological relationships for a minute. Who is your family then? Who are the people that surround you in your life? Put yourself in a movie. What would your story be? We may have mom and dad and siblings. We may have aunts and uncles and cousins too. Now, look at it differently. What makes you who you are? What makes your experiences on earth what they are and what gives your world meaning? Consider who contributes to your life experience and sense of identity. What is your family story with this enlarged cast of characters? How do the people in your life fit into your personal narrative, now and as you grow older? While family for sure can be thought of as parents, children, grandparents and all the folks on the relatives' end, three additional dimensions can help to define a broader sense of family.

First, a definition of family can include our entire network of loving connections. This network could include our immediate and extended family members, as in the traditional paradigm of family. But my research found that this "closed network" sense of family is shifting to an open network welcoming into the family bond close friends, mentors, even co-workers. We can get hung up on the idea that family consists of just family members. In place of a conventional definition of family, we seek a broader set of connections and the deepest of these define family. We must care for our ever-changing connections, which together add color and chemistry to our family soul.

In place of a conventional definition of family, we seek a broader set of connections and the deepest of these define family.

Second, this network of relationships is in a state of constant change, transforming and evolving over time. Some participants stay, others leave, some relationships intensify and grow deeper, others weaken and trivialize. The relationship mix and intensity are in steady flux. Like the seasons, the family is never fixed—it is in perpetual motion.

And third, family is self-defining. The best definition of family is whatever is right for you. If you are single and have a parrot, like one of my interviewees, and this is how you want to define your family, this is downright awesome. There is no

This network of relationships is in a state of constant change, transforming and evolving over time. Some participants stay, others leave, some relationships intensify and grow deeper, others weaken and trivialize. The relationship mix and intensity are in steady flux. Like the seasons, the family is never fixed—it is in perpetual motion.

"best" way, no wrong answer, only a prevailing sense of personal choice and self-acceptance.

One could ask: "What if I might consider someone as a member of my family even if that person might not consider me family?" Or similarly, what if one views his mom and best friend as family, but they do not consider each other family? In both cases it is not important that both or all parties similarly recognize each other as family. Why not take it one step further? Slice through the ambiguity by letting people know that you consider them family. In some cases, mutual recognition may occur just down the road a bit. If not, no need to worry. We are focused here on your loving connections and your self-defining, ever-changing network of relationships.

Extending the boundaries of family to include others brings large doses of vital and reverberating energy to the group. Long ago the soul of the family extended to the tribe or the village. Native Indian cultures, for example, were "gifted" with including the larger clan and its members into their family ranks. Think of council fires with elders, chiefs, clan mothers, medicine people, seers, counselors and historians—all sharing their viewpoints when the subject being addressed needed solutions or opinions. Family boundaries too can extend out to include others from the neighborhood, community and beyond.

For sure, there is a pressing need for an innovative definition of family. If we define it too narrowly, we have lost the contributions, inputs and rich diversity of others, who can add illumination, introspection, gratitude and wisdom to the family fire. We are social creatures and the family is the stage where we play out much of our lives. We wake up every morning and go to sleep every night with our family members or friends close by or in our hearts—not to mention those more geographically distant family and friends who live across the globe who require only a phone call, text, or email to come together. What resonated from my interviews is that today, family is quite simply whom we feel close to—who we love and who contributes to our sense of self. This love is best experienced when there is respect and trust for each other and when we connect honestly and deeply in our relationships. Importantly, when this respect and trust has been compromised but there is still love, the soul diligently works to bring members back together again.

Family, then, is an all-inclusive group of evolving connections. Some are hard-wired as is often the case with relatives. Others emerge along the way and are constantly changing and expanding. Family emerges by pulling in friends and colleagues from all sorts of circles over time.

Family, then, is an all-inclusive group of evolving connections.

Diversity in Family Make-Up

If I were to create a collage to convey the diversity of family compositions from those I researched, it might look something like this:

- A husband and wife with no children and several of their co-workers
- A father with three sons
- Two gay parents with two adopted children
- Siblings in a broken home

- A single woman and her co-workers and close relationships

- A man with long-time college friends

- A husband, wife, two children and their grandmother

- A divorcee with one child living near the former marital partner

- Two unmarried individuals with or without children

- One man and his iguana

The list of "mixes" can go on and on. The "traditional" family has evolved into the "transitional" family. Family makeup is unique, varied and defined by individual circumstance. At the same time, running in parallel to this refreshing diversity in family membership and structure are the evolving stages of family life.

> **The "traditional" family has evolved into the "transitional" family.**

Five Family Stages and Their Influences

There is a progression of family development *stages* that surfaced from my interviews. Our definition of family tends to transform as our family stages shift. Though, while these stages may appear to mirror phases of individual development, they are based more on meaningful events and personal connections than on the linear progression from childhood to adulthood. To clarify, life stages are more age/biological centric; family stages are more personal/relationship centric. The key idea here is that family is most often in a state of alteration and progression over time. The development may be a simple shift between two stages, the family you were born into versus the one you create through marriage. Or a person might only live within one family stage his or her life, choosing to remain in the family in which they were born. It could very well be that this person's concept of family did not change much in his or her lifetime (Stage 1). As we see in this example, family stage is not merely a function of age. More often, one's answer to "who is my family?" evolves over time and progresses through several different stages. Let's look briefly at each stage that surfaced in my interviews:

Childhood/Stage 1 – As a child, family might include parents, siblings, relatives, teachers, religious people, neighbors, school friends and pets—with, of course, good and bad influences in all groups.

Teen Years/Stage 2 – As a teenager, family might include friends (close and emerging), parents, siblings and school and extracurricular activity groups (e.g. sports, clubs, activity groups like the Boy Scouts, band, drama, etc).

Young Adulthood/Stage 3 – As a young adult to mid-life adult, family might include spouse or partner, children, coworkers or colleagues and of course friends and some relatives.

Adulthood/Stage 4 – As a seasoned employee and family member who may now have grandchildren, family may include aging parents and adult children, and of course close friends and engaged relatives.

Elderly/Stage 5 – As a senior, family includes close surviving relatives and old friends, plus all the memories that make a life complete.

Combinations of stages are also common. A person develops relationships with a collection of people at each family stage and, as they do, their sense of family changes. A sixty-year-old male interviewee shared who has been involved in his family over time and what that meant: "If you look at my family growing up, it included my mother, my father and my grandmother and me – that was it. It was the four of us, and Tad, the dog. Up until I got into the Boy Scouts, that was my family. I didn't have many friends, even in elementary school, because I was overweight. So then with Boy Scouts, that was when I ended up with a totally new family. That was a huge evolutionary shift for me."

Let's look at the influences in each period. In the first stage one may have relatively less control or influence and decision-making capability to determine family make-up. Family is defined for you; it is a given. It is the one you were born into. This can include bad influences too—an alcoholic parent, a bad teacher, or unsavory friends.

In the second stage, as a teenager, the family now shifts more to include friends—close friends and emerging friends. Parents and siblings, however, are often still present at this second stage, as they are still a source of interaction and engagement.

Stage three introduces a big shift; a family stage evolution occurs. Some people get married and have children and the spouse or partner create a family of their own. In others, friends and co-workers are brought into the family mix.

But look what happens at stage four. Many adult children begin to take care of their aging parents who have come back to be a part of their immediate family circle, just when their own grown children move out to start their families.

At stage five, very close relatives and old friends continue to serve as points of connection and support at this last evolutionary family period. Importantly, memories serve to recall past connections and influences.

A definition of family, then, is no longer simply one's relatives. Instead, it includes all those individuals to whom we feel close—friends, colleagues and favorite furry friends. We constantly care for these individual connections—strengthening and sustaining some, discarding and releasing others, and letting new ones take root. This network of diverse relationships is ever changing, self-defining and stage-driven. Across the developmental shifts and the many different manifestations of family, however, the soul endures.

❧

Today's family is a broad and deep network of interconnections and relationships. Paralleling this refreshing diversity in membership and structure is the continual metamorphosis of one's sense of family.

5. Applaud the Caretaker

"I was pondering a definition of the soul of the family and, oddly, I kept coming back to the grandly narcissistic idea that it was me! My husband talks about coming home each day to me; when something goes wrong in the family, my sisters call me to take care of it; when something goes right in my children's lives, they tell me to reflect it out to everyone else. I am the nerve center. My entire life is focused inward on the family. Even my work life [in business with a family member] is family-oriented."

—Interviewed parent

Keeping A Hold On Constant Change

Change in the family is ongoing and constant, like the ebb and flow of life. New family members arrive, children and parents take on new obligations, some move to different locations, experiences are shared, relationships change and the family expands and grows. Family members come and go in time, strengths and weaknesses grow and diminish and the family bond evolves. The caretaker attempts to keep track of, manage, and celebrate these changes!

Like any connection, quality time and effort cultivate deep, rich relationships. Closeness requires making sure to stay in touch with each family member, knowing what they are going through on a regular basis and being supportive and interested. It may be as simple as spending time together communicating and catching up.

Since the family is made up of different relationships, the soul of the family changes when family members change. For example, as changes occur in one's career—training, learning and growing each day – one is continually evolving into a new "me," and the relationship to one's family changes accordingly. Each interaction is shaped by one's daily experiences, one's perspective of self, of the world, of life and, thus, one's relationships with family members. At the core, family members still share their original bond, but each person carries individual experiences with them, and the family soul as a whole evolves with new life experiences, just as people do.

Championing the Soul

> **The caretaker is a champion for the soul of the family.**

The caretaker is a champion for the soul of the family. It is someone who pays attention to everyone in the group, the well-being of each member and the family's overall connectedness. The caretaker may initiate contact so others know what is going on, continually keeping them informed and updated. When family members are half a world away, this person may write a note or letter, send an email, or post a snapchat, and by this very small reassuring act, has the power to strengthen the bond of the overall family network.

Communication is vital to the family's sense of unity. The caretaker's role includes encouraging dialogue and information flow, rectifying that familial remark, "he never calls," with action steps.

The caretaker tries to make sure everyone in the family circle is cared for, or in the words of one such individual, is "able to go on joyously in their lives." The caretaker reaches out to touch others and creates relationships and, in doing so, is the hub of the soul of the family. The caretaker spotlights who could use some love and concentrates on delivering it.

This job becomes particularly tricky under our new definition of family that embraces relationship beyond traditional filial bonds. The issue might arise: How can my family have a single caretaker if not all family members consider each other family? When our family members are cobbled together from a broad spectrum of life experiences, it is the caretaker's job, along with any other vested members, to act less like an intercom system and more like a prism, radiating love across disparate family groups.

Based on my interviews and observations, we might think of caretakers as accomplishing five core tasks.

1. *Reaching Out to Others and Bringing Them Closer*

How does one connect family members who are spread out and side-tracked by daily life? What does staying in touch look like? One parent who does it *extremely* well shared her approach. It was something that she loved, and took over from her mother's cousin, noting: "I want to reach out. Grandparents should be called. Birthdays remembered. I send out special old-fashioned greeting cards to let someone know they are special and to keep in touch with them." She always tries to make it a card that would tickle a person, rather than a generic birthday card. While she acknowledges that people do this now on the Facebook "wall," she strongly feels that getting a specially selected piece of mail on a birthday can more profoundly hit the mark.

She reaches out to friends and "extra children" in the same way. All are part of her *modus operandi*. "I keep track of everyone and *always* their children. If I have a relationship with their children I want to keep that going so they won't feel left out." Again, she hand-selects an appropriate gift, and frequently offers to coordinate it with others, if friends or relatives want to join in. She notes that she takes on a lot of these types of roles—the ones that no one has time for but everyone appreciates. It is a role, she stresses, that she likes, and wants to play in her family.

2. *Managing the Diverse Needs of Family Members*

Being the family champion also requires keeping track of everyone and managing the family's growing number of needs. "I have multi-families. I have my family that came through my current husband, I have a family that came through my widowed husband, and now I have a family that came through my daughter and her new husband's family. I really feel like I have added a whole new set of family members that I want to care for and include." The circle gets larger when new folks are added to the circle.

There is additional expansive "work" that can unfold. When this mother's children were young, she often played the role of "editor" for their school papers. Now she finds herself editing her sister's books, her sister-in-law's speeches and her husband's articles. The circle of involvement and influence grows, given the type of professional skill set and abilities that she brings into play. This is common in families. We all tend to seek others out who are good at something, and the caretaker is frequently asked to help out and address the family's diverse needs.

3. Serving as the "Nerve Center Commander"

The caretaker acts as the nerve center of the family, keeping track of what is going on in the lives of family and friends—and sharing their successes. One family came up with an internet-friendly way to "reflect" back what they were proud of, encouraging children and adults alike to take part. They send out an email to immediate family and special friends and share a note that says "we are so proud of you," mentioning the recipient's specific accomplishment. For example, a mother reported that her son just won the county film festival award for best score in a commercial given to a high school student. Everyone then sent him an email. It served as a shorthand way for everyone to know what someone in the family did. One doesn't usually send it about oneself. A person would send one out about her mother/father, child, husband or friend, if something special happened to them. Family members report that they enjoy the news and, interestingly, the kids are especially glad that the information is shared. Not just an award, it serves as a way to specifically share what they are proud of about that person.

This same mother explained that staying in touch takes initiative, work and attention to detail: "I call my mother every day, I call my first widowed husband's mother at least once a week. I call my husband's mother a couple times a week when she is in Florida, and when she is here we see her at least once or twice a week. As parents get older it just seems like the way to go. I don't have a set time to call. I just call when I have something to share, when I am thinking of them. Then it is not a chore. Occasionally it is, like my Aunt Rachel, who has had Alzheimer's for two years. I took it on myself to call her every week just because I knew it gave her some joy."

Maintaining family closeness, then, requires staying in touch. A family needs a caretaker who *likes* doing it. It requires reciprocity. If one person makes the extra effort to reach out and create the opening, then another person has to be open and accept it. "I don't mind making all the extra efforts to make things work for everyone. There only needs to be the one person arranging the holiday grab bag this year." The point here: someone needs to play the caretaker role—set things in motion and open communication channels, so that closeness and connection will flow naturally.

4. *Organizing and Preserving Traditions, Holidays and Celebrations*

In addition, the caretaker's role may include executing and preserving holiday traditions and celebrations. "Holidays are important to me and to my family. My parents take charge of the religious ones, for which I am grateful. I always thought it was important to celebrate all the holidays, which happen cyclically throughout the year. These add tradition, festivity and joy. It can be as much fun as putting out vintage heart-shaped candy boxes for Valentine's Day." The caretaker makes these connections—is in touch—and becomes this kind of nerve center. "It is always coming from me going out—and it comes back obviously, but I get the pleasure of putting it out there."

> **The caretaker makes these connections—is in touch—and becomes this kind of nerve center. "It is always coming from me going out—and it comes back obviously, but I get the pleasure of putting it out there."**

Another soul caretaker described her efforts to preserve family traditions: "We use the holidays to express traditions that are important to continue because that is what keeps us who we are. That is one of the signals we have that identify us and make us unique." In many ways traditions define who we are as a family. Take Thanksgiving. One family can't not make mashed potatoes or grandma's chocolate pie recipe because that is what "we always make."

Traditions are not only a way to celebrate special occasions, but a way to celebrate the family itself. "They are what you do that make you unique. I do it differently than you do it. My family does it differently than your family does it," says one parent.

5. *Engaging in a Juggling Act*

Tending to everyone at once requires some skilled juggling. "I feel I have my brain and my heart in all these other lives. I want to help them stay balanced, stay happy, stay well, and do whatever I can to keep them in a good place. Sometimes it is very overwhelming. I have been adding even more family members, and trying to keep everything balanced is tough."

Being a caretaker is not unproblematic, nor void of conflict. Family members may be far away or located in entirely different regions, making connection and "upkeep" challenging, says one interviewee. Logistics, then, become a struggle for the entire family. Someone may see his or her family members more often simply because they are closer, which may cause imbalance. One member who missed seeing her mother said: "Robert's family is here, mine is away. I feel guilty that I don't get to see my mother as much." My research found out that often the adult child who is close geographically to the aging parent juggles the large number of growing needs and requests that come with aging.

Interestingly, one caretaker admitted that it was difficult to maintain balance when the adult kids returned home! While she loved having her children back, their arrival on the homefront tends to throw off her household equilibrium, making it difficult to focus on, think about, or accomplish anything work-related while she was in her own home. Talk to any parent who has experienced the arrival of the "gang" of returning adult children, single or married, along with their own schedules, significant others and even pets, and you will quickly understand. One parent concluded: "I like my adult children to live by me, not live with me!"

The Importance of Caretaker Transition

Every family can benefit from a caretaker who initiates and nurtures communication so that family members can interact and communicate with ease and frequency. When a family loses a caretaker, someone new needs to step up to the plate, or the bond may weaken. The job of caretaker of communications and traditions can be difficult to fill and caretaker transition can be crucial to preserving family unity. Someone—or multiple family members—must step in, accept the job and garner acceptance.

One person said that her sister was trying to keep communication going by putting out a weekly email after their mom died, but was receiving few responses. Relatives and extended family were far spread. Her mom had been the person who had told all of the six siblings what each were up to, and was beloved by all the cousins and nieces and nephews too. When there was an event at her place, everyone in the large family would attend.

More often than not, the caretaker role is taken on by new family members at each family stage. Over time, *different* individuals step in to keep connections thriving.

If no relative is available, a non-family member may even be the solution, as one now sixty-two-year-old interviewee explained. He described an ever-changing caretaker throughout his family stages. During childhood his caretaker was his grandmother. In his teen years his sports team served as his "family" and the caretaker was his coach. In college his friends were his family and, along with a religious mentor, they all became caretakers. During graduate school his family was a group of friends. During his very first and second jobs his bosses were caretakers. Now sixty, he is the caretaker, along with his youngest son (in his twenties) who has kicked in to be the caretaker, as well as several people from his work. As he gets older, he expects the caretaker role to shift again.

December of 1973

Dearest Mother,

This will probably be a very hard day for you, if this letter reaches you on Tuesday. I wish I could be home for quite a number of reasons, but mainly to be near you and the rest of the family. Physical distance is going to get in the way I'm afraid; so let me share a few thoughts that I hope will help you through the day.

Grammy seemed to always help us inadvertently through days. She radiated so much joy and love for everyone. It was her way of "giving." She gave those precious intangible gifts, whether they were her simple and wise words and beliefs, her abundant expressions of love, her big smiles (which covered her physical pain), her strong morals, and her loving and cheerful sense of humor. That is quite a lot for one person to share with others.

What I'll miss most is her incredible wisdom. I loved going up to see her and just listening the whole time; I learned so much from her about life and people, especially seeing the importance of a sense of humor. Oh! She was an amazingly beautiful person.

We all will never forget her. I only hope I can be like her. Just incredible she was with that huge sense of humor. We all will miss her, but her intangible gifts of love and humor will not go away. I'm sure she is happy now, just because she always was happy all the time. We should be happy because she is and because we got to be so close to her for so long.

Her impact will be forever with us. She embraced the world with her heart and for that reason will be accounted as the best. In her were the greatest beauty and the most profound love. She was void of greed and envy and malice.

If we can open our hearts as she did and fill them with the same gifts she gave us, we will have accomplished what she has done—to embrace the world with her heart and to give to others the beauty of love.

God be with you, mom. I'm thinking of you and my heart is with you.

Love and prayers,
Susan

Letter about Grammy.

Saying Good-Bye, Saying Hello

Sorting through our family house, I found a letter that I had written to my mom when my grandmother, or "grammy" as we called her, died at the age of ninety-three. Besides this original hand-written letter, still in its mailing envelope, there were sixteen copies of it, all organized in a separate file in the kitchen drawer. It appeared as though the letter was to be shared with others. I was unable to come to the funeral service because I was taking my final exams in graduate school. To travel from east coast to west coast was impossible (this was 1973 and the world was less mobile, particularly for students). Grammy had been the quiet caretaker of our family. While my letter (see sidebar) sums up what I mean, let me paraphrase: she radiated cheerfulness, humor, love—and happiness. A family's caretaker also serves as a role model.

The baton passed to my mother, who then became the caretaker of our family. She shared this role with several of her sisters. They did a remarkable job. And as they aged, others have stepped in to become the passionate and devoted champion for the soul of our family.

ويو

The caretaker is the champion for the soul of the family. Essential to the family flow and cohesion, caretakers accomplish several crucial tasks: they reach out to others and bring them closer, manage the various needs of each member, share what is going on in each other's lives, organize traditions and gatherings, juggle conflict and change and serve as role models.

6. Start A Family of One's Own

"I have lived apart from my parents and my brother for the past nine years. Whereas our family's soul is always present and eternal, I do think it feels weaker—at least to me—when I am gone for a long period of time. I feel my family's soul strengthens whenever we are all home and together. In a way, I view it like a cup of water, which can be replenished, or slowly evaporates if left untended for a long period of time."

—A twenty-seven-year-old interviewee

This same twenty-seven year old continues: "At the same time, I am recently married. I am now starting my own family with my wife. I feel like a new chapter has begun and my family's soul grows stronger as I begin to merge my wife and her family with the family that I've known for my past twenty-seven years of life."

Twenty- and thirty-somethings are a particularly important group when exploring the soul of the family. They are experiencing rampant change. Two gargantuan events often occur at the same time. Twenty- and thirty-year-olds are still part of their birth family *and* they are launching a new-to-the-world family. Significantly, the soul of the family is the glue that binds the younger new family members together *and* the same glue that connects them to their birth and extended family. The soul dangles its fruit—a sense of belonging, uncon-

> **The soul dangles its fruit—a sense of belonging, unconditional love, support, nurturing, and caring—and twenty and thirty-somethings are in for the picking. Their fresh voice and perspective adds to our discussion of soul.**

ditional love, support, nurturing and caring—and twenty and thirty-some-things are in for the picking. Their fresh voice and perspective adds to our discussion of soul.

Although the concept of a "soul" may at first seem abstract to this age group, if you chat with them, as I did in my interviews, they have no difficulty pinpointing the important role that soul plays within the family. Quite profoundly, they feel that in order to care for the soul there must be frequent connection opportunities. Specifically, they feel that individuals need to overcome geographic divides to care for each other's souls, and a family needs to be together for the family soul to feel whole. They weighed in on a wide mix of topics.

1. Changes Over Time—Birth, Sickness, Aging

I spoke with this age group first about family changes over time. Twenty and thirty-somethings understand that the soul of the family transforms through marriage, birth and death. One twenty-something said: "I think the soul of a family changes as new individual souls enter and exit the family. I also think that families can grow closer or far apart over time. If family members don't stay connected, especially if they live physically apart, the soul of the family can weaken."

The focal point that most strongly shapes the family soul changes over time. "When my brother and I were kids, I felt that my family's soul largely revolved around the two of us. This past year, my father went through a long bout of health problems, so I feel that my family's soul is centered largely on him. A lot of our family's love and attention is directed his way as we all help him gain physical and emotional strength."

He viewed close friends as being adjacent to a family's soul, as opposed to being within a family's soul. This makes sense. Time may have not yet allowed this age group to have lifelong friends, those rich and deep friendships, steamed liked a fine tea.

2. On Friendship

One interviewee explained that close friends in one's twenties and thirties can influence who you are and who you become as an adult, often in a profound and life-altering way. However, he viewed close friends as being adjacent to a family's soul, as opposed to being within a family's soul. This makes sense. Time may have not yet allowed this age group to have lifelong friends, those rich and deep friendships, steamed liked a fine tea.

3. Impact of Death and Struggle

When asked to share how one knows if the soul of the family is present, one twenty-something offered touching emotional detail. "A death of a close family member causes the soul of the family to be extraordinarily present. When my grandma passed away, I was twelve years old. Although I was a child, I did feel a growing understanding of my life, my place in the world, and my place in my family. I remember my dad crying as we buried his mother. My dad never cries. I felt his exact feelings of sadness and loss at that moment. It was very powerful. I could see it in my mom and brother's faces that they felt it too. Sometimes sad occasions are most powerful in bringing people together."

"Because of this episode, I have called my mom and my dad more times in the past four months than any four-month period while I've been gone from home in the past nine years. Although I am geographically distant from them, I feel closer to them. I think struggle and pain has this effect on people."

Nor is the role that struggle plays in chiseling the family soul lost on this age group. One twenty-something man describes his challenging family situation. "Last year, my father was diagnosed with a condition in which excess fluid builds in the brain. It affected his ability to walk, talk and remember. It has been very hard for the members of my family to watch his functioning deteriorate. Thankfully, there is a way to treat this condition, but it required several surgeries and lengthy hospital and rehab stays." He continues: "He hasn't been home in the last four months as he is still recovering. Obviously, this has been hard on my dad. But it also has been very hard on my mom. She has been his sole caretaker, and he's not always an easy patient. Because of this episode, I have called my mom and my dad more times in the past four months than any four-month period while I've been gone from home in the past nine years. Although I am geographically distant from them, I feel closer to them. I think struggle and pain has this effect on people."

4. Benefits of the Family Soul

One twenty-something identified four specific benefits of a sense of family soul:

- A sense of belonging
- Receiving and giving unconditional love
- A sense of purpose
- A feeling of freedom to pursue your wildest hopes and dreams

What more can be said about the *mega* impact of the soul for this age group? Let's simply leave it at that. This twenty-something has pushed through the clouds and seen the sunshine!

When asked if they ever experienced a family time when the mood was particularly heightened or intense, when they could actually feel energy radiating from the family soul, one twenty-something shared a beautiful description of this "spirit of us" force. "My wife and I love to travel. For us, it's the best way to experience new things, and experience the world. Our best memories are from faraway lands. This is often when we are at our peak happiest. It feels like adventure, excitement, being outside of our comfort zones, and experiencing things together for the first time."

Yet he qualifies these peak times, adding: "Of course, life is not all about experiencing new and wonderful things. Much of life is repetitive, and that is when we grow weary. However, we can find happiness in the mundane. I think if you are with someone you love, you can find happiness anywhere."

5. *Transitions, Personal Growth and Hardship*

Life unearths change, growth and discovery on the soul front, as this twenty-something details. "Over the past five years, I feel like my wife and I have grown as individuals, but more importantly, fused our lives together. I feel that my wife and I share a soul. I think this evolved over time as we spent more time together, made memories together, talked about our hopes and dreams, and took steps towards creating a family, such as moving in together, and getting married." He continues: " I think that once we have kids, this will be another major step in the evolution of our soul. And even though we will be adding a new individual to our family, I think our family will still have one soul. And it will be full of love as the strongest force that binds our lives together."

Family can be a safe place where members reach out embrace, comfort, applaud, cherish and awaken each other's powers and welcome everyone just the way they are—tears, fears, struggles, hardships and all.

Twenty-somethings agree. One interviewee substantiates this point of view. "My wife and I often joke that we accept each other warts and all because neither of us is perfect and we love each other regardless of what faults, fears or insecurities we may have." He shared an experience in which his wife had an important discovery. "My wife recently made a career transition that brought her to become a sixth grade social studies and language arts teacher. I've often thought that teaching, or some professional career with kids, is her calling. Caring and nurturing kids just comes so easy to her. And it fills her with happiness. Unfortunately, her first year as a teacher was a difficult one. She would probably describe it as a nightmare. Her kids were unruly, rude and cruel. She often came home crying. Pretty soon, she was strategizing about how she would quit."

Here is where the power of the family as a "safe place" or haven for hardships comes in. "Because she had her parents and me as sounding boards and support systems, she decided to tough it out. And we're all glad that she did. She is now in school year number two and she loves it. She learned a lot from that first terrible year, and has grown stronger because of it. But I don't think she would have been able to persevere without love and support. That is where the soul of a family comes into play. It's about knowing that you have people who love you, care for you and want to see you succeed."

6. *Supporting Each Other and Celebrating Togetherness*

One twenty-something commented on the role of the family in celebrating each others' successes, which can be particularly important for twenty- and thirty-somethings beginning their new journey as independent adults, career people and spouses. "I am lucky that so many people in my family are my biggest cheerleaders. My wife is my strongest support system, and she is by my side every step on my life's journey. My parents provide a constant source of encouragement. When my Grandma Harriet was alive, I always joked that she was my 'PR rep' because she was quick to brag about her grandson's accomplishments to the rest of the family."

"Sometimes it is as simple as sitting on our couch in our family room watching a favorite TV show. Or sitting around the dinner table, eating and laughing. To nurture the soul of our family, I don't think it matters what we're doing, as long as we're together."

He continues: "My wife and I make a point to try and spend as much time as we can together. I also fly home from time to time to see my parents and brother. When I'm home with them, we spend a lot of time together. Sometimes it is as simple as sitting on our couch in our family room watching a favorite TV show. Or sitting around the dinner table, eating and laughing. To nurture the soul of our family, I don't think it matters what we're doing, as long as we're together."

Twenty and thirty year olds are oftentimes members of two families—the "old" birth family and a new-to-the-world family, created and launched through new relationship building. The family soul acts like sticky glue, connecting them to both.

7. Welcome In-laws and Special People

"When we have Christmas Day, it is a family thing. Over the years, when a new boyfriend comes into our family, we decide as a whole whether or not that person would be invited for Christmas Day. The condition is everyone has to meet him in advance before we decide he can come for Christmas— or there is no getting together."

—Interviewed grandparent

Christmas is special. This family knows that. Protectively, they want to check out a newcomer before their holiday and have devised a system to do so. Everyone has a vote—and a voice. I like this system because every person is equal. Parents and daughters alike have an equal say as to whether or not their special holiday can be opened up and shared.

Now, let's take "entrance" another step—from boyfriend to more permanent member—how does one join the traditional nuclear family? The quickest, sure-fire, most literal way is to marry into the group. To be viewed and treated as a true member, however, is far from straightforward. In my own family, we call these in-laws "outlaws!" It can be hard to find acceptance in another person's family. My mom experienced this difficulty first-hand when she married my dad. Both came from larger families, six children from one and five children from the other, and each family was extremely tight and close.

Outlawed In-laws

To feel a sense of inclusiveness, my mom's strategy was to create an intra-family group of her own when she married my dad. Because there is power in numbers, she selected my Aunt Ann and Uncle Maurice to launch the new group with her, as they too were outlawed in-laws. It was a brilliant, innovative idea. The "Outlaws" were all the in-laws who had married into the extremely tightly-clad, secure family clan. With all the combined siblings and their married partners on both sides, the family roster was constantly increasing. Many new in-laws enlisted and gladly joined my mother's troop of in-laws! With a family so close, outsiders needed to be both included and empowered, and the "Outlaws" acted as a forum of sorts to let this happen. As she got older, my mom was referred to as the Outlaw's Chairman of the Board. When my husband, Tom, married me, he too became an "outlaw."

Encourage your family to establish an inclusive group such as this, especially if the family is extremely close. Feeling included is terribly essential to individual happiness, sharing and growing close together. Come

The Outlaws.

up with creative ideas to make this happen, even if you have to establish an "Outlaws" outpost. Note to family members: Be inclusive. Awaken to the fact that becoming a member is a difficult, lengthy process for outsiders coming in and that gestures that signal inclusivity are extremely valuable. You may be surprised how much the energy of outsiders enlivens the family soul.

Why Be Inclusive?

Inclusiveness means being recognized and accepted as part of a whole. Individuals who are inclusive are open and respectful of differences, fully embrace who they are as human beings and view others as a valuable part of the group. Family members who strive to be inclusive acknowledge and act upon the needs of others and communicate the value of their perspectives, thoughts and opinions.

Inclusiveness should be relatively simple to activate within a family, but for several reasons it is not! We seem to have certain biases and prejudices about others. As adults, we tend to exclude certain individuals more readily. When we do not understand others, we tend to feel inferior or superior to them.

The crucial requisite for inclusiveness is to deny all forms of discrimination—period. There are no excuses or rationalizations for being unfair to another person. At times, family members position themselves above the fray, making others appear to have flaws or deficiencies in order to make themselves look good. Often, the motive to exclude is subconscious. We need to become more aware of subtle exclusion. Inclusiveness means becoming conscious of our differences, accepting them, celebrating them, and then trusting others.

The daily life of the family offers fertile soil for this to occur. Cultivating the gifts of *all* those around us is one of the most powerful ways to move forward. The more family members make others feel included and valued, the greater the harvest to be reaped.

Simple Ways to Be Inclusive

Reaching out to let in someone on the fringe so they feel included can happen all too easily. Let's hear some first-hand perspectives on the gracious "invitations" that were extended to not only in-laws but family visitors too.

My dad took my husband Tom frequently for a drive out to his beloved land. The ritual involved getting into his old dusty pickup truck for the journey. The open back was filled with dirt-crusted "junk," old and odd type things, which Tom, who lived in New York City at the time, shared little knowledge of. Importantly, the land had a peacefulness that was difficult to replicate. The two of them soaked it up and, importantly, Tom picked up the warmth of my dad's inclusive act. The very first time they made the trip together was on the afternoon Tom had come for a visit to Oregon from a four-day cross-country bus trip, arriving without his forever-lost luggage. (College students traveled inexpensively in the early seventies by bus!). Our favorite dog, Jazzy, died that same afternoon of a heart attack and the two of them went together to bury him on this special spot. My father and husband were bonded together for life. As to my mom, she *always* sent cards and gifts to Tom, never missing a holiday or celebratory event. But more, he emphasized, my parents included him in conversations. While this sounds like a simple gesture, it created a powerful feeling of belonging. Both parents *always* expressed interest in his work and his ambitions, and here's the key—they would also share this information with their friends, which had a sort of domino inclusive effect. In Tom's words, "their friends also made me feel included—Hub and Erma, Jack and Phyllis, and on and on, so many of them. They all really made me feel so special."

Giving something tangible to a person can have an immediate "inclusive" impact too. Shares my book editor, Marci, who grew up on her family's cattle ranch in Oklahoma: "When I first introduced Jon (her fiancée) to my dad, my dad gave him a Jacobs Ranch pocket knife. Jon immediately felt like part of the family and like one of the cowboys." Similarly, simply giving someone a task can make them feel a part of the scene, as she shares more here: "Sometimes being given a role in a family event, or a simple job to do, can make one feel part of the family ecosystem. Last week I visited my blind friend Heidi who I hadn't seen in a couple of years. Her mom asked me to whip the cream by hand between dinner and dessert, while holding one of Heidi's cats in my lap—I felt one with their family, picking up right in the middle of the family chaos." Reaching out with a simple gift or getting one involved in the party are two powerful ways to "let in" others.

Getting Rid of Hierarchy

Let's underline this point: all family members are equal. And this includes in-laws and others invited into the family network of relationships. Some will find this a difficult pill to swallow! I believe hierarchy leads to more, rather than fewer, problems. Each person can have a voice and be a part of the family decision-making process. Now, you can never reach total consensus, you can never please everyone. But if a family can create a culture where there is transparency and openness, a sense of fairness and integrity can occur.

Here's the catcher: hierarchy isolates us from each other. It stifles the exchange of ideas and collective power of the family. And the limiting aspect of a rigid structure is not lost on family members, especially in-laws. When members know that there is no channel in place for their voices to be heard, they often retreat from the family altogether. There must be a way for members to contribute, to say: "my ideas and thoughts all went into the decision, my inputs got included, and the outcome was something that I was a part of."

Sadly, exclusion reigns in many families. However, when inclusiveness exists, individual members feel attached and connected. They know that they belong and play an important role in the growth of the family. They are involved in shaping the family culture. They know that their comments are heard and their contributions are valued. Family members should be able to say: "I listened to everyone; this is what I heard; this is what I am doing; and this is why I am doing it." This creates an inclusive family.

One Family's Success at Inclusiveness

Let's take a look at two family situations: The first hits a home run in inclusiveness and we can see its positive impact on this family's soul. In contrast the situation described in the subsequent section describes a family in which exclusion and prejudice had pierced a hole in the hearts of its family members.

First, the success: One introspective interviewee shared the following scene of her "enlivened" family home front when "other" family members entered the group. "My mother-in-law and stepmother have both been strong influences on how we have shaped our family expression and expectations. We have had hilarious shared extended-family moments together." She explains: "We were on vacation with my entire husband's clan; during our visit we celebrated our niece's thirtieth birthday. All present were uncomfortably aware that my mother-in-law was suffering from some type of memory loss (she had shown up for the vacation week with no money and a bank card she had cancelled herself several months before)." What transpired was something to hoot about: "It is still hilarious to see the look on my niece's young face when she opened her birthday gift from my mother-in-law, a DVD entitled 'Yoga for Seniors.' There was a moment of shocked silence, and then we all laughed until we cried. To this day, we are not sure if my mother-in-law meant it as a joke, or simply missed the 'seniors' part of the title."

Her stepmother too is a strong part of the soul of her family. "She is the most easy-going, optimistic, flexible and generally non-judgmental person that I know. She has taught us all to say 'Love Ya' and is the 'mother ship' of family hugs. She has weathered family arguments, helped my strict father to soften his edges over time, and offered insights or just 'balance'—mostly from fifteen hundred miles away, but as often on holidays as we can make it happen." She confirms: "Exposure to her has had a clear impact on my two children and me, and they know that they can express themselves around her without being shut down. There is ease in the relationship. She is an outstanding Scrabble, cribbage and card player, so we have all learned to suck it up and lose to her – and we have an awful lot of fun doing it."

Another Family's Failure at Inclusiveness

While inclusion was a windfall above, it didn't work too well in another family, where differences were not respected. The soul of this family has suffered immeasurably, as we witness here: "I am Catholic and my husband is Jewish. His parents did not want him to marry me but finally came around. Interestingly, I come from a very devout practicing Catholic family who had no issues with me marrying a Jewish man; his family did not even belong to a temple. If I asked his mother about certain Jewish traditions or practices, she would never seem to know the answers."

She continues, "It's hard coming into an extended family knowing that there is a part of you that is not accepted. When I was pregnant with my first daughter, we wanted to be honest with his parents; our plan was to raise our kids Catholic and baptize our daughter. His mother's response was that she would rather be dead. Although I love my in-laws, their refusal to accept or be a part of the religious part of my daughters and me make it difficult to ever feel truly connected with them." She concluded, "They like to 'pretend' that our daughters are Jewish, and tell them that it's never to late to get bat mitzvahed or that they should go to the Hilo house on their college campus."

Her family conflict is made more intense by a secondary challenge: "My husband has one brother and their relationship is very difficult. Younger and very competitive with my husband, my brother-in-law got married shortly after us, and he got a divorce right after we had our first child. He has told us that he didn't feel like we were there for him when he went through his divorce and, to this day, still holds a huge grudge even though he remarried and has one daughter." She continues: "The biggest issue is their mom, my mother-in-law. She fans the fire all the time between them. My husband's brother always likes to proclaim that he was always mom's favorite. To this day, if we go to his parent's house for dinner, his mother cooks his brother a whole different meal of his favorite foods, which is different than what she serves everyone else."

More upsetting details: "The brother's daughter was just bat mitzvahed and I made sure we did everything we could to show our support. (If I left it to my husband, we wouldn't have even gone to Shabbat service the night before or bought her a beautiful necklace). At the Bat mitzvah every single relative *and* friend was called up to the beama at one point, *everyone* except me, even the new husband of a cousin who they had never met and who was also Catholic." She said that the entire two front rows were empty with the exception of her. "My husband was very upset and felt they were punishing me because of his relationship with his brother. Whatever their reason, it just reinforced for me that as much as I love his family, we will never be able to take it to a deeper level because there are too many grudges. There is an inability to be truly honest and sincere with each other."

Whew! For sure, the related conflict is not good for the soul of their family. Weakened because of this ongoing arduous situation with her in-laws, their family bond is under constant stress. Feelings of rejection surface and intensify.

Inclusion Is Imperative

Every family, then, has the "other family" or those folks who have joined the family circle through marriage. Extend family membership to include these remarkable individuals. Family making must involve a well-meaning reach out to include individuals into the family ranks who are not related by blood. It is difficult for in-laws to feel like a true member of a family. Admittedly, I still check-in and look out after my husband at my family's holiday events. As unique members, "outlaws" can feel at times excluded, even if we never mean to omit them. Open up the membership, welcome in-laws and special people, including boyfriends and girlfriends, into your inner group, and your family will deepen for years to come.

❧❧

Welcome in-laws and special people into your fold. Inclusiveness can be infectious. Removing family hierarchies allows members to participate and share of themselves more freely. All family members are equal and this includes in-laws and others invited into the family network of relationships. Some may find this "welcoming" a difficult pill to swallow but the reward is worth the effort.

8. Bond with Multiple Friends

"Many people will walk in and out of your life, but only true friends will leave footprints in your heart."

—Eleanor Roosevelt

"There is a joy in seeing everyone together. There is sharing, laughing, and the dogs barking and racing around with excitement that broadens and enriches 'our' family, swelling the spirit and energy that is our normal. The addition of different ages, personalities and talents enriches the whole in a palpable way and on so many levels. The sharing, listening, supporting, respect, acknowledgement, sympathy, empathy, and depth of history are huge. There is frank discussion among the young of current events and respect for differing views. It is an enlarged circle of love and encouragement to take away, hug tight, and help with the unevenness of life. It is a giving that gives back tenfold."

—Interviewed parent

"It is an enlarged circle of love and encouragement to take away, hug tight, and help with the unevenness of life. It is a giving that gives back tenfold."

Aptly put, friends expand and ignite the spirit and energy of the family soul. Don't miss out here. Extend an invitation to a friend or two. It truly "gives back tenfold." Echoed another interviewee: "I don't see the soul of the family as reaching out to others—I see the soul of the family as inviting others in. Some stay a short time, others a long time. Some stay until they are connected to and part of that family."

Close friends, then, can be extensions of a family, but they have to be invited into the core. Just as family members shape the social relationships and interactions that make up the soul of the family, close friends too help to deepen our sense of who we are. Like family, friends are integral to an individual's inner learning, growth and happiness. Note how family members will ask about one another's close friends when catching up, just as friends inquire about family members. For sure, friends extend the family boundary outward and the soul of the family is infused by their energy and love.

Some families are more prone to involving others in their family scene than others. And they are wise for doing so. The more participation and connection that we get from others, the better, don't you agree? This is especially true at critical points in our lives, such as raising children and teenagers—when we feel we just can't do it alone and need all the help we can get!

Reaping the Benefits of Adding Friends

What benefits do friends bring to the home front? The gathering of family and friends infuses the family soul with revitalizing energy, intelligence, fun and humor. Friends enrich the scene. Often, in our own small world,

> "I see the soul of the family as inviting others in. Some stay a short time, others a long time. Some stay until they are connected to and part of that family."

> When we are stuck in old patterns and habits, friends can help us climb out. They can enrich the life of a family, deepen it immeasurably, and add joy, change, and new perspectives to the scene. Rather than a dinner of four, think of a twenty-five foot long buffet table in the dining room and you get the idea.

we fail to consider or miss something. And friends, well, they can come in with the answers, just when you need some help. When we are stuck in old patterns and habits, friends can help us climb out. They can enrich the life of a family, deepen it immeasurably, and add joy, change and new perspectives. Rather than a dinner of four, think of a twenty-five foot long buffet table in the dining room and you get the idea. Friends enlarge the scope, the choices and the answers to the challenges that face family life. Friends are essential to the growth of the family and its members. Friends connect us with what's important. We need their support and guidance in caring for our families and each other.

DON'T MISS THE FOREST
FOR THE FAMILY TREES

Valuing Inclusiveness— Widening the Family Circle

My mom loved parties, people, popcorn, pickles and her daily program—physical and mental. It consisted of three meals, a daily morning work out in her bed (this was smart—get it over with!), and what I will call "mind exercises"—a crossword puzzle and Jeopardy most every day. Importantly, she had friends in about every corner of her life. These are people with whom she had close relationships, who were *not* technically family members. She managed to stay connected to friends from her earlier days. To get a full feel for their astonishing variety and influential power let me categorize. She had her bridge group, neighbors, bowling club, sewing group, dance club, college best friends, golf group, small town connections, in-laws, travel buddies, colleagues from work, my dad's work group, her own kid's friends' families and the now-infamous "Rogue River Gang"—an annual river rafting group of twelve buddies. Quite remarkably, my mom was continually on the lookout for new friends. And she *always* brought them into our family mix. It added brilliant and fabulous energy, not to mention loads of laughter, to our family frontline.

> **Quite remarkably, my mom was continually on the lookout for new friends. And she *always* brought them into our family mix. It added brilliant and fabulous energy, not to mention loads of laughter to our family frontline.**

While a close family was vital to her, so was pushing out the boundaries to include others. Inclusiveness was located at the top of her values list. It seemed like we *always* had someone living in our basement growing up. Let me mention a few "add-ons": Mike, who was the son of one of my mom's closest friends in life, was like a third brother to me (he lived there four times); Tom, who became a priest; Sally, my best friend from college days; another Tom, from Sweden, who spent the summer working in the local cannery; and Nota, my friend from Greece, who came to visit the Pacific Northwest. We often went on spring vacation with an "extra" in the car. Picture six crammed in one of those 1960s large, long, always-white

> **It seemed like we *always* had someone living in our basement growing up.**

sedans (dad thought white cars were safer), three in the back and three in the front seat. Inclusiveness was paramount.

One might ask: What exactly did my mom do to make those "invited in" feel included? Mike, our family friend who slept in the sofa bed down in our basement the most had this to say: "I always remember the sense of family that was there. It was odd, but there were not a lot of rules. We were never sat down and told don't do this or that. There was an unwritten language that said we all cared for each other here. And absolutely *no* one intrudes on that. One time we excluded a boy who was two years younger when he came over. We could tell we did because he moped off. There was never any scolding, but it was very clear that we had done something wrong. She told us that when people come to this house we could *never* make them feel bad. There was a sense of her putting her arms around everyone, sort of like a giant hug feel, and we all are here to make the people in this house feel good when we're together." He reflected more: "The interesting part was that there was never a verbal or physical hug. She just made you feel the hug. The more you acted out (i.e. weren't behaving), the tighter she hugged. She had this aura or presence: she held tighter and tighter until you didn't act out, all without making you feel bad. It was like come here, settle down, everything is going to be okay, and when it was over, you better go out to play now."

> **"This kind of love cannot be scripted."**

Inviting Others In

The benefit of opening up the family to include others is, well, gargantuan! As one parent stressed, "Why wouldn't one want more loving people in your life?" My own mother would certainly concur. For certain, inviting others into the family mix makes for a livelier scene, added fun and a much needed "help out" with raising children and teens.

Adolescence in particular is a time of confusion and contradictions for teens and parents alike. Close friends can provide the gentle, enthusiastic support parents need to help their teens develop strength, become independent, and grow into responsible adults. And when young adults are ready

Another family friend, Sally, who lived with us for three months after we graduated from college, also felt a permeating sense of inclusion. We both worked in the local fruit and vegetable cannery that summer. She explains: "I grew up in the suburbs of Chicago so of course had little knowledge of how vegetables got stuck in cans! When I came to spend the summer in Susan's home with her parents, I was instantly included in their family life. They even gave me my own room with my own bathroom! There was a comfort, a familiarity and assumption that I was one of their own kids. Bula and Farmer (as I called them) were wonderful, kind, loving parents. The love and respect they had for each other carried over to the way they treated their children. I was miles away from my own parents and siblings but I always felt loved, included and supported in whatever we did."

She continues: "They both showed an interest in listening to me, and they listened intently, and then remembered things that I had talked about. Also, the sense of humor was so evident. If there was some kind of kitchen disaster like smoke coming out of the toaster, problems were dealt with and life kept going. Meals were fun, informal and there was never any rush to hurry things through." She adds: "We were all-business while at work during the day at the cannery, but returning home, most evenings we would sit outside in the backyard while Farmer would delight in playing bartender. Our college days of drinking beer were set aside while we joined them in the beautifully crafted Old Fashioned cocktails with a side of cheese and crackers. It was fun, it was 'grown up,' and once again we would sit and talk and just enjoy each other's company. They always took the time to share love, show their interest and discuss thoughts and ideas."

She reminisces: "One evening we went out and visited Susan's high school friends, and stayed out a bit late. We were back home safely, laughing, talking and carrying on probably a bit too loud for a household that was already sleeping! Bula knocked on the bedroom door, peeked her head in to see what we were doing and said in a cheerful, friendly, but firm voice 'Goodnight Susan!' It was a loving reminder that we were being too loud but she was still glad that we were having so much fun. That summer, she had two daughters that she shared her love with." Concluding, she reflects: "The day came when it was time for me to return home. It was a summer filled with adventures, great laughter and memories. I truly felt like a family member. And as I was busy trying to avoid saying goodbye, Farmer got a little misty eyed, which made it even harder to leave. We had shared our lives, shared our hearts. This kind of love cannot be scripted, faked or demanded. This kind of parenting came straight from the heart."

to "launch," friends can share in a collective "whoop" about their arrival at adulthood.

One of the parents I interviewed explained that her family has two close friends that have been included in *all* of their family gatherings, including vacations. Her mom took a summer course in arts administration and met Ellen, who was smack dab age-wise between her own mother and her and her three sisters. "My mom brought home this friend who was so cool wearing hot pants. How could this be my mother's friend?" The friend has remained an important force in all of their lives, sometimes called their fifth sister. Her own daughter asked her to sign her wedding contract because it couldn't be a relative.

Life tragedies also expose the need for the inclusion of friends within our family network. This same interviewee explained that her family included Michal in their gatherings. Michal had lost her two brothers in a fatal plane accident. So when her own family became smaller, she was integrated into their larger family group, not only for holidays and vacations, but for daily phone communication too. These two women, now invited into the family group, have become close themselves and vacation together.

Simply put, close and loving family friends share and experience the great adventures and great sorrows of life with us. Using kindness, empathy and good humor, they speak to the heart and get to the heart of the matter. They can serve as a wise and supportive guide to each family member.

Viewpoints on Adding Friendships to the Family Mix

A grandmother of three told me just how important friends are: "Since we don't have family nearby, we have friends who are part of our family. We have a crossover—a lot of children of our friends are our friends, and our friends are their friends…These friends are just like family." She traces this back to her first year of their marriage, when she and her husband left Minnesota and moved to Michigan and Illinois and needed to make friends. She reveals: "We never went back home [to Minnesota] for Christmas and it was hard because we had huge family traditions. We made up our own customs. A couple of weeks before Christmas we baked seven different kinds of cookies. Then on Christmas Eve we dressed up, packed up the cookies and visited friends from work and our theater group, staying for twenty minutes or so at each stop." Most people were having a holiday event at their home, she explains. After a visit with each of their friends, they went out to dinner, just the five of them. She reflects: "We got very lonely the first few years away from our extended families in Minnesota. But our new tradition helped us. Visiting friends from our newly formed connections added to our family circle." Importantly, friends got to know their children as they were growing up from these annual yuletide visits, eventually followed by other year-round get-togethers and events.

Another person shared her personal story: "There have been so many friends. Of course, one of the first to come to mind is my friendship with my college girlfriends, which we've had for forty-three years. It continues to nurture me, and hopefully them as well. This is a group of similarly aged peers with whom we have been able to share our lifetime experiences of getting jobs, more education, travel, marriage, raising families, supporting each other through hard times, such as losing parents, and happy times, like anniversaries and graduations, and mentoring each other." She adds: "There have also been those older generation folks who have acted as mentors and were great friends as well. Now many of them are gone, which makes the family traditions change because they are not here anymore. I no longer can count on the big fun effort of cleaning up from the huge holiday parties around the kitchen sink and listen to their opinions on life or their stories about former lifetimes. And I miss that. But that's life: ever-changing."

One Family's Story—
Serendipity of Friendship

How does one become a member of the family group? How are the boundaries extended outward? How are others invited in? Is there an actual invitation of sorts? It can happen so easily, if you let it! Let's look at how one family "invited" others in. My friend, Reven, shares how she met her closest friends, those that gather every year for their Thanksgiving feast. She and her husband, Reed, ran into a couple, Bob and Cathy, at parenting classes after the birth of their first son. On a stroll while pushing through the alley with her six-month old son (and dog), she met Lauren, emerging to dump her garbage, who quickly decided that the baby boy would be perfect for her baby daughter. Unknowingly, the two children would grow up together. She met another couple while they were working on the Oz Park playground project. Nancy was a graphic designer and agreed to do all the PR in their joint efforts to build a community playground. Nancy's husband, Herb, was struggling to get through a math course and Reven's husband, Reed, stepped in to coach him. The two women became close friends, and down the road, fine art painters, sharing a studio together. She met another friend, Johanna, at the farmers market and, while this was the initial link, each family had a son on the rowing team. Each of their two boys became best friends, as did the parents.

As time passed and life went on, Nancy's husband died of a heart attack. They all grieved together, helped her through this deepest of struggles and their bond stretched and strengthened. Nancy continued to come with her sons every Thanksgiving. Lauren and her husband divorced, but she too continued to come with her two children, a girl and a boy, who loved their two boys and were loved in return. When Nancy died after a two-year battle with ovarian cancer, the entire group took over the surrogate-parenting role for her two boys, now fully employed men.

To conclude, the beautiful words of Kahil Gibran in *The Prophet* hit home: "Your friend is your needs answered. He is your friend which you sow with love and reap with thanksgiving. And he is your board and your fireside. For you come to him with your hunger, and you seek him for peace."

৵৩৵

Friends ignite and expand the spirit and energy of the family soul. They are integral to each member's inner learning, growth and happiness. So invite, include and involve others in your family scene, and treat them as family members. Friends enrich a family immeasurably.

Parents and children alike, I was told, look forward to their Thanksgiving feast more than any other celebration. Here's the scene from one family's "joint" celebration: With time and age the boys grew at different heights, a cause for ribbing and as mustaches grew from faint to more noticeable, they were a cause for more ribbing, and a kind of hilarity that only boys seem to muster.

Then there's the Thanksgiving food. Bob makes an always-delicious 22lb. turkey, the gravy from scratch, and the stuffing, so rich that Reven's son would dream and talk about it during the year. Because Bob took the leftovers home, Reven started making her own turkey, but smaller, of course. A healthy competitive streak developed between the two chefs! Bob made mashed white potatoes and Reven made garlic sour cream red skin and Yukon gold mashed potatoes and French green beans. Nancy made the salads. Reven made the pies: apple, apple/peach, apple/peach/pear, then strawberry/rhubarb, and of course the pumpkin pies that always had ground cloves that contaminated the coffee grinder for weeks after.

Their feast had a predictable routine. Shared one family member: "It was about the "entrance." Bob coming in with his pots of steaming gravy, the turkey, the cold air, the rush of immediacy, the delicious smells, the hellos, the women hugging the women and commenting on hairdos, dresses, the boys hugging and hitting each other." Their routine also included the "anticipation of the first to arrive, the preparation for days before, the sharing of the cooking, the deciding of the dishes, the excitement of picking up *Betty Crocker* with her mom's recipes and her art teacher's illustrations in it."

Their unique celebratory routine was described in more detail: "We greet, we talk, we drink, we eat, we rave about the flavors, and we groan from over eating. The younger set descends to the basement. The older set groups, chats, gossips. Someone plays the piano. It is cozy, comfortable, predictable and so much fun." She reflects: "Thanksgiving is a combination of anticipation, of remembrance of past friends and family, catching up and sharing of current exploits, adventures, and academic and professional goals, relationships current and ended. And problems. And breakups. And sadness. It swells with the kid's current girlfriends and boyfriends, or a friend who can't make it to his or her family, or is without a family, or the enchantment of a grandchild running around, fixing an eye on you, and asking frank questions." Their holiday gathering reached out to include friends, creating a swelling of spirit and energy that enlarged the family and embraced its soul.

9. Discover A Soul Friend

"One soul friend has helped me and our family throughout the years by helping me put things into perspective and suggesting options in a non-judgmental way. Just knowing that she is supportive and is there for me if I ever need her gives me strength. It is important not to lose your positivity when faced with life's struggles and this soul friend reminds me of that through the example she sets with her own life."

—Interviewed family member

"I do have a soul friend. He was my college roommate freshman year and continued on as my roommate or housemate for the next seven years after that. We are very close, and we're always rooting for each other to succeed and fulfill our life goals. He has invited me into his family, and I have invited him into mine."

—Interviewed twenty-something

In *The Sacred Path Cards: The Discovery of Self Through Native Teachings*, author Jamie Sands notes that in sacred traditions wealth is measured by a person's ability and willingness to help others in need. The "selfless" individual she is talking about might be considered or is what I like to think of as a soul friend. A soul friend has achieved a higher level of knowledge and understanding of us, or has a spiritual life that lends them a profound capacity for caring, or is simply someone willing to help others and serve as a teacher. Soul friends help guide us along life's arduous path.

Do you have a soul friend? If the answer is "yes," feel fortunate because they are precious and often rare. Soul friends are different from soul mates, those difficult to find, sometimes-perfect partners, although soul mates can sometimes be soul friends. A soul mate is someone you actually share a life with, whereas you and your soul friend are on your own life journeys, cheering each other on while carving out each one's own unique path. Soul friends can be long-time friends who check in on you and inspire you. They are the type of friend who can pick up a conversation as if it were yesterday, even though you haven't seen him or her in a long time.

He or she is simply a close friend who loves you for who you are. You can discuss anything with them without holding back. They too are often exploring their own life path and gladly share the details of their own journeying. There is no competition or threat between you. Their purpose is simply to aid and abet your life course. Soul friends give without expectations of return and don't seek recognition for their attentiveness and involvement in your life. In their mind, success is not measured by your position, possessions, or wealth—only by your happiness. While a soul friend may be aware of your struggles to succeed, he or she admires qualities you possess independent of life successes. A soul friend is a close companion who is consistently encouraging.

Soul friends are one of life's rare treasures. They are friends of the heart with whom we share an intimate connection and a special bond. When we look back, they have often healed our hearts, reconnected us and fortified us to continue undeterred on our journey.

Soul friends are one of life's rare treasures. They are friends of the heart with whom we share an intimate connection and a special bond. When we look back, they have often healed our hearts, reconnected us and fortified us to continue undeterred on our journey. Soul friends are deeply dedicated to us and partake of our celebration of life. With gratitude, we can acknowledge their role in our personal learning and growth. We can individually thank these people who allowed us to call on their "personal medicine" when we were in need.

Teachers and Friends of the Heart

At the core, a soul friend is both a companion and a teacher, someone who we can feel more fully ourselves with and who encourages us to be our best selves. A soul friend is an inspirational model. We all have important people who have given us guidance. I interviewed family members about the presence of such a soul friend in their lives. Most everyone was able to identify such a person and describe how this "over-the-top" individual had an impact. They portrayed their soul friend as an extraordinary person and companion who deeply encourages and supports them, and always lends a helping hand and listening ear.

Some are lifelong friends and family members, some are friends we make along the way by happenstance, some enter our lives at critical times. Shared one interviewee: "Soul friends help in different ways. The struggles we've faced as a family have put us in contact with others who have similar struggles and I have found that by being vulnerable, by being open and honest about our struggles, I have given others the opportunity to teach me." She continues: "Everyone has struggles and I truly believe that there is something for me to learn from every person in my life. I think when we help each other individually, when our hearts are open to the thoughts and teachings of others, then the individual growth we experience furthers the growth of our family."

This interviewee believes that self-knowledge is the foundation for all knowledge and she is grateful to have friends whose wisdom has guided her toward deeper self-exploration. She added that she too has dear friends and family who are "stuck" in their lives and in their struggles and can't or won't move forward. She in turn offers them love, support and wisdom, deepening her own experience in so doing.

How Soul Friends Help

Weighing in on the unique power of her soul friends, one person reflected: "I have eight soul friends. Each one is helpful to me in a different way. It depends on what I want to share, a joy or a concern, as to whom I might call. One friend is good at encouraging me, one is good at challenging my mind, or challenging my body, one is candid, one can listen, one

Here are a few more examples of soul friends: "It's funny because I would never have thought that this person would end up being my soul friend. We've known each other since we were fourteen years old. We haven't always taken the same path. We were friends in high school, but I went on to college." She explains: "Our different journeys were not without struggles, which could have kept us from being friends. But through our good and bad experiences, we've forged an everlasting friendship. We like to say to one another, 'we've been through some things.'" Continuing, "We don't have to see or talk to each other on a daily basis, but we are there for one another at all times, as well as our families. When we do talk, it's for hours. We are always mutually encouraging and uplifting. Our conversations are very spiritual. This was *not* how we spoke as teenagers or young adults. We've grown into our spirituality through our experiences."

Another shares the power of a soul friend: "My husband has a first cousin, who is twelve years older than we are. She has three adult children, and she was a nurse. She lived through some difficult challenges growing up, developed a terrific sense of humor, and picked up wisdom and insight along the way. When we were having trouble with our youngest son, I talked to her. And I talked to her before I summoned the courage to ask our oldest son if he was gay. She connected me to an LGBTQ group."

How did she describe this soul friend? "She could tell when I was worried, and said to call anytime. She checked in on me to see how I was doing or how was it going. She was encouraging, wise and funny, was great to have in your corner, been there to a certain extent, but didn't presume to say that she knew it all, or that her experience will be your experience, but had enough insight to know that everybody is different."

can question." In sum: "All of them help me find clarity and strength for being with and helping my family. At the core of our relationship is honesty and caring. They are part of the soul of *my* family."

A husband talked about his wife being his soul friend on the family front: "My wife is a wonderful, naturally gifted mother and I feel that I have learned to be a better father through her example. She has always believed in me in over thirty years that we have been together. Her support and encouragement have been, still are, and will always be invaluable and cherished."

Similarly, a wife talked about her husband, who served as a soul friend within their family: "My husband helps enormously with our family. His sense of humor and perspective were invaluable when we were raising our two girls (now in their thirties) and still provide a steady, even keel for us all."

Offer Sage Advice and Serve as Sounding Board

Soul friends are exceptional individuals. They often provide sage advice, an experienced ear and a fresh perspective, idea or solution that you may not have thought of yourself. There is great comfort in sharing the details of a problem. All kinds of information can be exchanged without fear of evaluation or judgment. Soul friends often serve as a sounding board—not rushing in with the answers, but instead giving a road map or hints to help along a difficult family path, ensuring personal discovery and ownership in overcoming life's challenges.

As adult children get older, soul friends are often needed more than ever to step in to help with a fresh perspective and much-needed guidance. One mother shared a remarkable story of how her daughter sought advice from a close family friend, Sam, who came up with a resourceful solution when the daughter got a one-half point too low GPA. "Let's figure out what to do," Sam said. He told their daughter to talk to her college professor to see how she could bring up her grade. The professor admitted she received a B- because of poor spelling and raised her grade a half-point. Later, the last semester of college, she received straight A's, even though she had a newborn baby and a job. It was the soul friend who had stepped in with a creative solution. In my opinion, soul friends are creatures from heaven.

One Family's Very Treasured Soul Friend

Let me share a touching story, told to me by an interviewed parent, of her family's extremely long relationship with a soul friend, from the extraordinarily colorful beginning to her passing. The parent conveys an enduring, magical friendship and intense bond that enormously impacted her entire family over the years. I purposefully have preserved the details of her story, as they convey the depth and adventure of their connection, infused with humor, emotion, togetherness and inclusion.

"Ordella Ida Hilda Geisler Hoffman, otherwise known as Giz, was the first female veterinarian to graduate from Kansas State. She came from a large German Lutheran family outside of Hebron, Nebraska. We met Giz because she was our family vet when I was a little girl.

My family enjoyed visiting an old-fashioned dude ranch every summer outside of Jackson Hole, Wyoming. It took two days to drive there. About a month before our departure, my dad said he could not go with us because of a court case in another state. My mother, Pat, who never let anything get the best of her, decided she would find someone else to go with us. So she asked Giz, who was single at the time and in her forties. We didn't know Giz socially before that time, although I guess my mom had seen her here and there with mutual friends. Amazingly, Giz said yes. About two weeks later, my dad announced that things had changed with his legal business and he could now join. What to do? We asked Giz if she would still like to come, and she did! On that trip we became fast friends and we would share everything with each other for the rest of our lives. The friendship began by taking picnics in the car because that's how Giz travels. Part of the adventure was trying to find that perfect picnic spot, which could have taken longer than eating in three restaurants.

On our first day of travelling in *very* hot July weather, one of the station wagon's tires blew out. So dad stopped to change it. About an hour later, another tire blew out. So dad and mom hitched a ride to Mullen, Nebraska, to get help, leaving my brother and me and Giz to fend for ourselves in a field of unplowed hay with nary a tree in sight. The only shade we had was from the triangular piece of shade we got from a windmill next to a livestock water tank. We helped ourselves to the water, cooling ourselves off with Giz's wet handkerchief and contenting ourselves listening to Dr. Giz's animal adventures.

Giz would end up becoming my parents' best friend and one of my best friends. She was a second mother to me. She would be at our house for dinner nearly every night, when Dad was in town or out of town, bringing over vaccinations when the dogs needed them (and the dogs always knew when she walked in that she had them in her purse and would scurry away.) She would be at all our holiday parties, even after my parents died. She helped me with my wedding, she helped me with my kids, she helped me with my parents when they were falling apart and she was falling apart herself due to aging and eventual illness. She would call me nearly every day to see how I was doing. When I was having a difficult time because there was no diagnosis for my invalid mother until three weeks before her death, Giz would tell me that it was okay—that I had done everything I could do and nothing else could be done, that 'old dogs' couldn't be fixed. She would encourage me in my marriage, encourage me about my children and that I was doing a good job with them. She'd rant with me over how my eighty-something-year-old uncle wouldn't make a will, and she'd take me and my family and friends out to dinner for my birthday.

When I could see she couldn't continue to live in her own home independently after a small stroke just after my mother's death, I had my father write a check as a deposit on an apartment in his retirement center so she could live there. My friend, Gayle, helped me to encourage Giz to make the move.

When my father was dying of pneumonia in his bed in his apartment and I had two young children at home, Giz scooted me out one night and said she would sleep on the couch in his living room. She was my angel that night, as my father passed away with her there, and I knew that he knew he was not alone.

And when she suddenly got pneumonia herself, I was able to round up my husband, son and daughter in thirty minutes (none of whom were at home) to reach the hospital in time to say our goodbyes, with Giz pushing her hand out of the covers to hold our hands. The next morning my AFS (American Field Service) Intercultural Program sister Sriyani and I went to pray with her. We talked about all the good times we had shared at dinners, at the ranch, in places we have travelled to, and how much fun it had all been—along with the Old-Fashioneds. Her relatives walked in, we said we'd be leaving to let them have some time alone with her, and would be back later, but looked down to find she was no longer breathing. I knew we had done the right thing to come at that very moment we heard she was so sick, and we all felt deeply privileged to be there with our angel Giz."

Their souls touched once again, for the last time.

Soul friends are deeply dedicated, exceptional friends with whom we share a very close connection and bond. They can heal our hearts, reconnect us and fortify us to continue undeterred on our journey. Often acting as teachers, they inspire our personal learning and growth. They may give sage advice, an experienced ear or simply a fresh perspective, idea or solution. Holding off evaluation or judgment, they serve as a sounding board, or a road map, to help us along a difficult family path.

10. Add Pets to the Scene

"We have two daughters and two female cats that are also siblings. Something very unusual has happened in our family. Our two girls have observed the way the two cats interact and have actually modeled and changed how they relate to each other. They told me that they are better sisters by watching how the two cats get along."

—Interviewed parent

A pet's influence is *enormous*. Pets teach us about unconditional love and acceptance and, in this sense, they are truly wise instructors! They also provide comfort, compassion, connection and centering for the family. No wonder we panic if they disappear or get lost, as the iguana story illustrates below. They also help teach responsibility, provide a focus for love and caring, and give back affection and trust. Pets deepen the family bond and, in this sense, are truly integral and soulful additions. A pet has a personality of its own and brings a sense of livelihood, creating an enduring bond between family members.

Pets, then, play a significant role in becoming a happy family and shaping the family soul. They help us get closer and hold us together. How do they accomplish this hugely important "task"? Through their loving and accepting way, we find and experience unconditional love. We learn from our pets both how to love and how to accept. No matter what we do, our pets are there for us, tail wagging. Sharing a deep, loving relationship with a pet is enthralling and truly one of life's great pleasures.

They also add a wonderful sense of simplicity to the family scene. Animals are a source of love without all the complexity of family dynamics. Consider this equation: human family members equal love plus complexity; animal family members equal love plus simplicity. This is especially true in homes that are steeped with deep family tensions, addictions and other complexities. Pets offer a peaceful space to get away from troubling dynamics, yelling and stress.

Personal Stories of Intrepid and Epic Pets

Pets ground families with humor, stories and love. Growing up, pets were a *really* important part of my family. Altogether, we had six cats (three of them named Dinah), sixteen kittens, four dogs, one lamb, a few rabbits, ducks, chickens, tadpoles and a turtle. We always included them in our family play. I can vividly remember setting up a pulley to a rope and basket so we could regularly haul our five kittens high up into our tree fort for the entire day. One of the funniest pets we had was a frolicsome lamb named Frisky, whom we inherited from my uncle Doug's farm. One day he got loose and danced all over the neighborhood before we could catch him. After that and other similar incidents, it was decided that "Old Frisky" would go back to the farm.

Another "escapee" that we had was a turtle named "Sam," given to me by Walter Norblad, who was our Congressman from Oregon. He brought Sam across the country in his car, and let him sleep in the bathtubs whenever he and his wife stopped. He found him in his backyard in Virginia, and he had quite a trip from Washington D.C. to Stayton, Oregon. We only had Sam for a short time, because he got loose and headed straight for the creek.

Looking in my mom's very old leather-bound birthday book, I recently discovered, along with all the names of new babies, aunts and un-

> **One of the funniest pets we had was a frolicsome lamb named Frisky, whom we inherited from my uncle Doug's farm. One day he got loose and danced all over the neighborhood before we could catch him. After that and other similar incidents, it was decided that "Old Frisky" would go back to the farm.**

cles, and best friends' birthdays and anniversaries, were the names of our cat Dinah's kittens (Mity, Tootsie, Smity and Bootie) on April 10th—along with our cat Holly's kittens (Itsy, Bitsy, Teeny and Weeny) on April 16th. Relatives, friends and pets shared birth date listings. This says something significant. Think too of all the pets that adorn holiday photo cards that families send out every year, and you get it: Many families *include* their pet as a vital member of their family.

Our golden retriever, Finnigan, is my cherished companion. He is an energy source in the routine of my day. We always have to take a walk in the morning. Same route. He knows it like the back of his paw. He bounces along at a fast clip, even though he is twelve years old. We see a variety of people and places, some attention grabbing and others not, and always try to soak up some nature. Routinely, he anticipates where he has been given treats on our past walks, pulls on the leash, and makes a dash towards the door of stores where "handouts" were provided. He never forgets a location! One of the shops moved—a post office where he was given treats is now a pharmacy. Still, Finny dashes to the door of the now-pharmacy, hoping for a delicacy of sorts. This customary walk is how I like to start my day. It puts me in a better, more balanced place. And better still, I have a companion along for the trip.

Beloved pet, Finnigan, wearing holiday reindeer ears.

Family Pets—Caring and Comforting Companions

We receive an annual Christmas card from a family who has lots of pets. Here was their roundup: "We said goodbye to some animals this year, Mataan, the most wonderful horse ever, now grazes in Elysian pastures. He came to us when he was six, and stayed 28 years. He taught many children to ride and was good and patient with them all. Long-time cat, Al, pushing 19 years old, also moved on." He continues: "But it wasn't all goodbyes. We hired two four-month old kittens, Leo and Louie, as rodent-catchers-in-training. Minutes after being let outside, they successfully launched their new careers. At their first performance review they were promoted to Cats First Class and given permanent positions. Our other cat, Jim, apparently told Leo and Louie that the retirement plan is pretty good, and that gave them added incentive."

My friend Sally recently sent me a photo of her dog, Henry, from her iphone. In the shot Henry is finishing off her ice cream, one of his favorite foods. She says that Henry practically breaks a leg when the freezer drawer opens, hoping that it is ice cream time. We give our own dog ice cream on his birthday. He devours it in all of three seconds, as we would gobble up a bowl of popcorn or a special cake. Sally sends me another photo of Henry and her watching her favorite television show together. I send her one back of Finny now sound asleep on his bed. At the risk of appearing a bit goofy, my point is: How we love these dogs! Pals and key members of our families, they truly are.

> "At their first performance review they were promoted to Cats First Class and given permanent positions. Our other cat, Jim, apparently told Leo and Louie that the retirement plan is pretty good, and that gave them added incentive."

My sister-in-law recently sent me an email. "We are getting a new puppy tomorrow, another Havanese like Bella [their current dog]. I admit it is a total empty nest thing for me but Lacey [their youngest daughter leaving for college] really wanted to be part of the puppy time so we are getting her now." She concluded: "That way, she will be housebroken and ready for hiking this fall! Paul [my brother] and I regularly fight over who gets to snuggle with Bella in bed anyway and that way there will be one for each of us. Weird, I know!"

Not so weird. Let me share with you our own morning wakeup routine. We usually hear an odd sounding "snort" and look up to Finnigan wagging his tail and staring at us from his soft deep dark eyes. You would think we were in love—and we are! If we show no signs of movement, he puts his paw on the bed covers, then makes a very loud shake sound, as though he were wet, and if this still does not influence us to get up, he subsequently sneezes.

Not only are pets, then, companions and comforting to boot, they help create family. Listen in on one interviewed parent and what she had to say about how pets "create" a sense of family on her home front. "When our four adult children left and created their own homes, they all got a pet. One son is now getting a second cat to keep his first cat company. My husband and I have become the grandparents of these five animals! We have a relationship with all of them even though they are in our kids' homes and located in other cities. I see how really important a pet has been in creating a family unit."

One interviewed twenty-something shared the role that his pets played: "I think pets can become a part of a family's soul. I know they have in mine. I grew up with two cats, Hoover and Disney. Then a dog named Paprika. In a weird way, I always viewed them as brothers and sisters—just furrier. Maybe it was because we were always around the same age. Or maybe it was because I had such unconditional love for them. I know everyone in my family did too. When they passed away, I experienced the same sense of loss as losing a human family member."

Communication and Connection

Pets are superb emotional communicators. They add to the family's emotional frontier. Some pets are more loved than others, but each brings moments of joy and humor to the group. "When we had Jake, the kids really had such mammoth love for this dog. It would be one of the things they would come home to see. Sure, they want to see their parents, but they were coming home to see Jake. He was soulful." She continues: "I was looking at some photos and realized there was something beautiful about that animal. There was a feeling of depth and love when you looked in his eyes. Our new little dog now is just a clown. It is a completely different relationship. He is so much fun, but it is not the same kind of relationship or soulfulness that our other dog had. My dog now, when you look in his eyes, he is trying to think, 'How can I get a treat?'"

Consider too: Pets bring a beautiful simple connection, void of argument, to the family scene. Shares one parent: "When you start having arguments with your kids, the dog is not going to argue with them. The dog is just going to be there. You know your kids love you, but they are difficult, or they are angry with you, thinking, 'My parents are on top of me to get stuff done.' But the dog is just there to be there. And I think it is lovely to have that in a family. I am glad we did."

There are different kinds of pets, not just the cuddly kind. I had a goat growing up. She was amusing and fun to watch, and provided a totally different connection. People have relationships with their fish or turtle or parrot or iguana. I have a colleague who has had a parrot for many years. When we get together our conversation always zooms in on his parrot, Veck. Person-like and emotional, the parrot gets mad at my friend if he spends too many hours at work, hides in the kitchen cabinets to avoid getting a bath and loves to play in cardboard boxes. The two of them are family.

The Adventures of Lost "Beardie"

Our ten-year-old neighbor shared the loving story of her iguana named Beardie, the Bearded Dragon, bought as a baby, only seven inches long. She affectionately described what happened when Beardie was about one year old: "I was walking him on his leash, when I received a phone call. I left Beardie on the porch and forgot he was there. The little beast somehow removed his leash and hurried up the lawn, all the way across the street into the neighbor's yard. We searched every bush, rock and blade of grass in our yard ten times over and still could not find him."

Worry about food supply, cold temperatures and neighborhood animals ensued. Beardie had proven to be a good hunter in the past and the weather was not too cold and rainy for a lizard. The roaming neighborhood pets, however, were problematic. "Our street had an abundance of dogs, not to mention cats. Our own cat had often tried to hunt poor Beardie on his walks around the house, but had never quite been successful. When attacked or threatened, Beardie would flatten himself like a pancake, exposing his painfully spiny backside. He would also puff up his throat and hiss to show his teeth." Long story short, her iguana was eventually found. "Beardie was sitting on the tip-top of a bush, munching his meal worms and lettuce [set out to feed him]. His chin was splattered with red liquid, so I guess he'd eaten our cherries too. As we stood gasping, Beardie licked his chops and gave us a rather knowing look. We took him down to the pond to catch him some fish for dessert."

Animals center the family. One mother noted that she felt pets were the precursor to children when her grown children were starting their own families. Her adult daughter took in an abandoned dog with lots of barking issues. Every once in a while, she would ask herself: "Why did I do this? Do I have to keep doing this?" The daughter learned that pets require a lot of effort and work just like their human counterparts. I think we say the same things about our kids at some point!

A deep loving relationship with a family pet plays an enormous role in shaping the soul of a family. Pets help us get closer and hold us together. We learn from our pets both how to love and how to accept. Who would think a wagging tail would teach us some of the most essential lessons about communication, connection and unconditional love!

PART 2

Tapping Into the
Soul of the Family

11. Fortify Your Family's Heart and Soul

Every family is on its own journey in tapping into its "heart and soul," or its fundamental essence. My research surfaced six soul strengtheners that can be used to connect and give a boost to family members. Think of these as family soul "vitamins." The more of each you experience and absorb, the more you strengthen your power of connection and the greater access you have to the soul of your family.

H for Humor

E for Emotion

A for Acceptance

R for Renewal

T for Togetherness

S for Struggle

> **Think of these as family soul "vitamins." The more of each you experience and absorb, the more you strengthen your power of connection and the greater access you have to the soul of your family.**

Each of these six experiences fortifies the soul of the family. *Humor* strengthens individuals and families; laughter has both mentally positive and physiologically gratifying benefits. The expression of *emotion*, happy as well as sad feelings, permeates and serves as a poignant bonding source. *Acceptance* of self and knowledge of each person's different strengths and values encourages individual development and self-expression.

A sense of *renewal* is felt when we nurture the powerful energy of family love, and fuel it with food, music, play, traditions, travel and community service. When the quality of *togetherness* exists, we find commonalities and are committed to the whole. *Struggle* is ubiquitous and unavoidable, yet it can make the group stronger. Together, these qualities create an enduring bond, internally and eternally.

The Difficulty

Getting to the point where family life is soulful and deep and truly satisfying is not easy in today's fast-paced world. A simple reality is that the soul often gets lost in our chaotic lives. Many parents and children, and friends and co-workers, feel disconnected from each other. Many just don't know how to put the six experiences to work in the life of their group. Picture the powwow within the Native American culture or the circle of covered wagons parked for the night as our ancestors traveled along the pioneering trails, and you get what many families are missing—a place to gather, exchange ideas, offer support, connect, and feel refreshed and restored.

Take out your kaleidoscope and look once again through its lens. I want to help you bring into *focus* the six simple ways to tap into your family's soul. Each "frame" or guideline was gleaned from insights from dozens of research interviews.

Picture the powwow within the Native American culture or the circle of covered wagons parked for the night as our ancestors traveled along the pioneering trails, and you get what many families are missing—a place to gather, exchange ideas, offer support, connect, and feel refreshed and restored.

- *Add doses of daily humor.* Laugh often, long and loud. Laugh until you gasp for breath. And if you have friends who make you laugh, spend lots and lots of time with them. Discover that when you make someone happy, it will make you become happy too.

- *Elevate and celebrate emotion and find ways to evoke it.* Happy energy is powerful. Celebration is an act of the soul. Every family possesses the ability to find merriment. Consider vacations, trips, special celebratory days, holiday gatherings, reunions and game playing—and don't forget to pull the plug on the tech equipment.

- *Accept all family members and create a safe haven.* Each person has unique qualities—and these traits create diversity. Accept all family members, regardless of differences. Learn to love them, just as they are. Accept yourself unconditionally. Fight against self-criticism, listen to your inner voice and try not to judge. Family can serve as a refuge for learning self-acceptance.

- *Identify specific activities for renewal.* Use food, music and travel to fuel and restore. Celebrations, get-aways and community service also create occasions for renewal, as does play, traditions, coming together and sharing memories.

- *Make togetherness tangible.* Create quiet times of togetherness—and noisy ones too. Make a big deal about grand celebrations—holidays, birthdays and other special days. Use food as a unifier. Discover your own togetherness formulas and tap into your creativity to find bonding ideas.

- *Find the silver linings in struggle.* Struggle can strengthen or weaken a family soul. It exists everywhere and comes in many forms. It can be episodic or enduring. Sometimes struggle ends in detached love—or it ends in joyful resolution. Almost always, struggle can provide insight. Unresolved struggle eats away at the family soul.

- *Celebrate the Harvest.* Acknowledge the gift of each other, express joy and appreciate the growth of each person in your family—and share individual accomplishments with all!

Twirl your kaleidoscope for the last time to witness ten "frames" or tangible tools, like those that emerged from my research. Each tool helps families think and *do* differently.

- **TOOL #1—Use the Three "S's"—step back, seek balance and simplify.** *Step back* and observe. *Seek balance* by using your whole brain to draw your family together. *Simplify* your life to conserve your energy.

- **TOOL #2—Re-create and play often.** Be sure your family engages in physical, creative and unconventional play. Let children show you the joy of living in the present. Tap into their expertise, as they put a playful spin on the wonderment of life.

- **TOOL #3—Speak from the heart.** Find an emotionally gifted star within your family and use this person to teach "heartwork." It is simply *that* important for children, teens and adults to learn to express their feelings, speak from their hearts and master the lessons of emotional intelligence. Empathy and compassion make an *enormous* difference.

- **TOOL # 4—Nurture equality and appreciate differences.** Value and nurture every individual within your family. Discover each other's strengths, cultivate equality and respect the different types of intelligence that each brings to the group. Appreciate that each person is smart—just in diverse ways. Encourage each personal life path.

- **TOOL #5—Praise descriptively.** Recognize the difference between descriptive praise and global praise. Give frequent and specific praise, as it motivates and facilitates learning and self-discovery. Remember: descriptive praise and advice works miracles on adults too!

- **TOOL #6—Record memories.** Make family imprints and create memories together. Tell stories, make movies, take photos and save correspondence to share favorite moments from your past. These memories bring happiness and connection, strengthen the family bond and liven up the shared history—often with comic amusement. In remembering our past we invigorate the soul of the family for the future.

- **TOOL #7—Identify family values and rituals.** Talk about your family's values, prioritize what is important to each member and seek consensus to generate a shared family value set. Understand the role that culture plays in a family and use this to create enduring family rituals.

- **TOOL #8—Listen selflessly, talk deeply.** Renew, improve and practice your deep listening skills. Selfless, compassionate listening is a prerequisite for sharing ideas, feelings and values—and is critical to developing meaningful relationships. Talking deeply creates a rare and powerful *energy*. Close and healthy families are built through frequent, honest, two-way talk with one another—and lots of it!

- **TOOL #9—See the change.** Whether long ago or in the present, transformation and challenge are a constant reality. The influence of the family's caretaker, members and soul experiences are pervasive and ever-changing. Be open to these shifts in the family dynamic and learn to grow with them.

- **TOOL #10—Be forgiving.** Know that the soul is at work when there is forgiveness. Forgiving family members, a friend, or colleague opens the door to positive energy and intention. Allow humility to permeate your everyday activities—and it will produce a remarkable result too.

The soul of the family often gets lost in our fast-paced, chaotic lives. Six experiences fortify the family soul: humor, emotion, acceptance, renewal, togetherness and struggle. These soul strengtheners can be used to connect and give a boost to family members.

TOOL #1:
Use the Three S's—Step Back, Seek Balance and Simplify

At the onset, use these 3 S's on your family's soul journey. *Step back* and observe. *Seek balance* by using your whole brain to draw your family together. *Simplify* your life to conserve your energy. You will be astonished at their powerful impact.

Step Back and Observe

Our youngest son, who is now twenty-four, taught elementary school in Jinmen, Taiwan. Visiting him was an eye opener, not just because he speaks Chinese. Taoism is practiced there. Next thing I know, I'm hooked on some of its themes. It is an ancient philosophy of living in balance and in harmony with nature. It's not about trying to get something or somewhere: It's about acceptance. Taoism teaches that wisdom lies in not contending. The secret is to allow things to take their natural course. The message for family members and parents is clear: don't fight against the current, flow with it. If we can learn to stand back, young children, teens and adult children will move ahead, following their own inner nature. Often, parents lead most effectively by permitting their children, of all ages, to be their own guides.

Taoist thought says to let negative forces pass through you—and to counter negative forces with love. Meeting hostility with kindness can be a helpful strategy for parents. Negativity emanating from children or adult family members may have originated as an attempt to reach out to you, becoming tainted as it filtered through one's personality and modes of expression. One must learn to look beyond negative expressions to find the wellsprings of love that are the living source of emotion and interaction between family members. Only then are we able to maintain our center, as hard as it may be, and to respond with love. Taoist thought says: Produce the right loving action at the right time. Timing is everything.

Tai chi is a martial art that comes out of Taoism. It expresses Taoist principles through the beautiful, flowing movements of the practitioner's body. When I take my walks in the morning with our dog, I always see a woman practicing tai chi, her body, arms and legs swaying in rhythmic harmony. The movement in tai chi is generated not so much in the forced exertion of muscle strength as in the consciously directed flow of chi (energy). Chi circulates through the entire body and enables one to move with ease and power.

With every move, the body appears to be light and agile. Grace, balance and timing are critical in tai chi—just as they are in relating to children, teens and adult children. In tai chi, force (i.e., muscle strength) doesn't matter. It is actually in yielding to force that we overcome it. Parents can learn to yield to a child's, teen's or adult child's oncoming force or blow— whether verbal (e.g., a nasty comment), psychic (e.g., mentally cruel treatment), or even physical (e.g., a misplaced fist)—and stay centered, retaining dignity and equilibrium. Here's how: Practitioners of tai chi strive to avoid something called "double-weightedness." This is your state when your weight is planted in fixed balance on both feet, and movement doesn't flow freely. To prevent it, tai chi uses the technique of stepping backward as the opponent advances, then stepping forward as the opponent retreats. This is the little sapling's stance as it bends to accept the fury of the storm and survives, while the old oak, rigid and immense, is violently uprooted. Don't be like the stationary oak, resistant and static. Rather, step back. This will help you weather the tempest as your child or teen storms into adulthood or your adult children assert their own point of view.

Practitioners of tai chi believe that one should bear oneself like the eagle that glides peacefully on the wind—until the instant it plunges from the sky to snatch a fish from the river far below. The eagle's restful alertness and its capacity for swift, decisive action are traits we parents would do well to emulate. Waysun Liao in *T'ai Chi Classics* describes it this way: "When in stillness you should be as the mountain: stable, peaceful, formidable, being yourself. When you are in motion you should move and feel like the waters of the river: roaring ceaselessly, yielding to any condition, capable of being both peaceful and powerful." The message for parents is to stay balanced. Keep a clear, centered mind. Conserve, rather than expend, your chi. Then, when you need to engage the roaring river or the striking eagle, your chi will be available to you. You have stored your strength for later use.

Keep in mind these images from tai chi. Discover the hidden power of the young sapling's nonresistance. And, in the restful stillness of the gliding eagle or the silent mountain, conserve your power and energy for use when it is truly required. Practice the art of yielding and of peacefully reserving your energy, engaging it when there is a need to respond decisively and powerfully.

Balance Both Sides of the Brain

The brain is two-sided, each half possessing a different style of thinking and a different energy. The left brain is the "know-it-all." It is the master of expressing itself logically, verbally and in written words. It is analytical, rational, objective and detail-oriented as it focuses on each step in any process. The right side is sometimes called "the silent partner"; it expresses itself randomly, through rhythms, patterns and pictures. It is visual, intuitive, subjective and overview-oriented as it focuses on the interrelationships between the steps in any process. The left side is time-conscious and the right side is timeless. The left side is linguistic, while the right is artistic. The left side is aggressive, while the right side is yielding.

Betty Edwards, in her book *Drawing on the Right Side of the Brain,* shows us the power of using both hemispheres. She believes that everyone can draw, even those who don't think they can. First, she asks her students to draw a picture of Picasso's "Portrait of Igor Stravinsky." Then she asks them to turn the Picasso portrait upside down and draw it again. When the students compare the two drawings, they find that the right-side-up one is quite poor, while the upside down one is rather good. Edwards offers the following explanation: "The left brain refused the task of processing the upside-down image. Presumably, the left hemisphere, confused and blocked by the unfamiliar image, turned off, and the job passed over to the right hemisphere." The left brain is forced to admit that the right brain did a better job.

We often ignore, at least within our Western society, this "right brained" way of thinking. Take a look at all the how-to books available. Most of them focus on the left-brain aspect of living, or how to evaluate and change behaviors. But relationship building is a whole-brain activity. The energy of the left side says "take charge," while the energy of the right side says "flow." If we learn to balance the left side with the right side, what might happen to our families? I believe we can learn to use both sides of the brain and "draw" families that think and express emotion openly, freely, and heartfully. Helpful mantra: Use your *whole brain* to draw your family together.

One parent shared his intuitive approach: "We care for the soul of the family by caring for the individual connections that are made—strengthening and sustaining some, discarding and releasing others, and letting new ones in. I guess the only way to do this is intuitively. I don't think any of this is left-brain. You can't say, 'now I have fourteen connection points, or I have two connection points, so that means I have plenty.' I actually think when people first fall in love, and just have that one connection point, this may be inclusive enough."

Simplify

The "channeled whelk" is the first shell that Anne Morrow Lindbergh describes in her famous book, *A Gift From the Sea*. It is one of my favorite books. This shell once housed an animal, a whelk, which has now run away. Its tracks are left behind and you see a winding staircase where the whelk used to be. The bare shell is stunning.

The message here is: *simplify our space*. Our house, like the whelk's, must be simple and tidy. We too must shed. Discover how little we really need to get through the day, not how much. Start with simplifying our outward life, our home—our shell. Engage in some "spring cleaning." The working mantra is: If less clutter, then more nourishment, more time and more energy. The goal is to make our home bare and beautiful, simple and tidy. For helpful guidance, consult the guru of simplification, Elaine St. James. She has written three books on this topic. Her thinking has infused and inspired mine and may inspire you to make some major modifications.

> **Discover how little we really need to get through the day, not how much.**

Then move to your inner life. Do some emotional cleansing here as well. Get rid of emotional negativity. When you do, you will become lighter and your intuitive track will open up. This newly cleansed emotional state will open the door for meaningful new experiences.

Shedding looks something like this: We work less, get rid of clutter and enjoy life more. We listen to our inner voice, enjoy solitude, do nothing, create joy and love a lot. We relax, switch gears, become more aware, make each moment alive and have more control. Shedding allows our more soulful state of being to come out.

The point here is: When we switch gears and make some shifts, our relationships grow and change. We must get rid of the things that get in the way of deepening our bonds. Concentrate on a *new list* of things that help you take more time for each other, enjoy the interactions this new time creates and communicate more deeply.

Elaine St. James suggests a number of ways to switch gears. Applied to your family, they might include: Get up early; eat breakfast out or take a picnic breakfast and watch the sunrise; walk, bike, take a bus to work or drive a different way; grocery shop early, even try a different store; meet your kids or partner for lunch in the park; pick up dinner at the local deli and picnic in the park at sunset; let the laundry sit for a week or find someone else to do it; postpone household tasks; take a vacation day midweek with your kids or partner and just play; exercise differently—at a new place, time, or with different people; take your work to a new place— cafe, new office, desk or library, and unplug your phone for an entire day! I'm sure you can add your own if you apply some creativity to the topic.

Make a list of the things that complicate your life, then start to minimize and eliminate them. Concentrate on a *new list* of things that help you stay loose and relaxed, take more time to enjoy, keep your energy level up, free up leisure time and make your career a constant source of joy.

When family members simplify, not only will they have more time, power and energy, but they too will become more creative. They will be freed for personal growth. Don't forget to teach children how to simplify too. Involve them in the shedding process. Every family member needs to learn how to conserve energy when they can, so they can release it when they choose to. Simplify and shed. Your soul will jump with joy. And best of all, your relationships will deepen and flourish.

❧❧

Use the three S's on your family's soul journey. Step back and observe. Seek balance by using your whole brain to draw your family together. Simplify your life to conserve your energy.

12. "H" for Humor—Add Doses of Daily Humor

"One of my favorite things to do is make my wife laugh. I think that is because laughter was a very important part of my upbringing. My brother was always the class clown and the family comedian. My dad has a very dry and sarcastic sense of humor, which has largely shaped my sense of humor. And my mom has this laugh where her whole head and neck flings forward with delight. It's infectious. I think laughter, and all feelings associated with laughter, is one of the best fruits that come from spending time together."

—Recently married twenty-something

There is no sweeter fruit than laughter! Yet ironically, it is not easy to laugh!

Consider recent laughter research and the medical benefits. Here are some stats. A news report came out several years ago that said children laugh approximately four hundred times a day while adults only laugh about fifteen times. Social scientists who have studied humor want to better understand why 385 laughs vanish. For sure, most everything is humorous to young children. They don't discriminate. They laugh so much that it's easier to note the things they don't laugh at!

These same laugh researchers also noted the medical benefits of laughter. Giggles relieve stress, control pain, lower blood pressure, provide an aerobic workout for the diaphragm, improve the body's ability to utilize oxygen and maximize the flow of disease-fighting proteins and cells to the blood. For health reasons, it sounds like adults need giggles more than children do. Laughter strengthens the insides, physically and emotionally. Our insides need these emotional releases, and it appears that daily doses

Funny Family Anecdotes

We hoot with laughter every time we retell this story about my oldest brother Dean leaving on a trip. His packed suitcase sat outside on the ground near the back of his car. But during the distractions of saying goodbye, he forgot to put it in the trunk before leaving. Much to our surprise, when he drove down the carport hill, he ran over it! He quickly realized what had happened, got out, threw it in the back, and drove off down the road, as though it was a common practice. We never let my brother forget this "accident" of sorts, and howl and whoop with uncontrollable laughter every time we retell this story to family and friends.

Playing the trickster is another way to let loose the laughter. My middle brother Paul can never find his socks. His youngest daughter is constantly hiding them in hard-to-find places.

Similarly, our family gets a bit extreme on April Fool's Day. The first person who calls with an April Fool's story or joke experiences a rather grand accomplishment. Now alerted to this day of trickery, the receiver must quickly phone other family members to tell them a newly crafted different joke before they hear form the first person, lest they lose this once-a-year opportunity. An added benefit, each "victim" on the first person's call-list gets a heads-up to launch his or her own plan on the remaining others. Picture an unstructured, impulsive chain of goofy story swapping, quickly snuffed out if someone beats you to the call. As soon as the word is out, it is hard to pull off a trick. Admittedly, each other's made-up stories are cause for friendly competition. Every year someone usually comes up with a remarkably creative (and often fittingly foolish) story that is something to chuckle and hoot about.

Humor was *very* important to my mother-in-law, who was a lifetime subscriber to the Erma Bombeck approach to parenting, which says that a sense of humor is key to survival. If nothing else comes to mind—just laugh. I learned that her son used to frequently throw oranges into the clothes washer, which was conveniently located next to the refrigerator in their kitchen. Picture the oranges turning to slush if his mother was busy in another room and missed the distinct rolling sounds of the first cycle!

Then there's my mother. She makes the best dill and sweet pickles in the region. She has always washed the large volume of handpicked cucumbers in her clothes washer. It shortens the pickling process dramatically. In fact, the local newspaper featured her unique technique and included photos of our washing machine. Imagine how embarrassed I was as a teenager to show this article to my friends! When our machine had to be replaced after many years, we had to consider the availability of a "gentle wash cycle" for pickles in our next model.

of giggles are best learned from children. Put differently, we all need to bring out our inner child, and when we do, others will join in the fun.

Here is a family of sisters who have mastered how to do it. "I remember one time when both my sisters came to visit and we just spent the entire weekend hanging out, goofing around and laughing. It's a memory that will stick with me. At one point we started having races to see who could scoot across the carpet in a rocking chair and I remember just laughing so hard my side hurt and I couldn't see because I was crying so many tears." She concludes: "This was definitely a time when I felt that bond and feeling of 'us'. It is these times when my sisters and I are able to just hang out, be silly girls together and just enjoy each other's company."

Removing cucumbers from the clothes washer.

Whooping

There are funny stories in all families. A sense of humor is vital—use it! And don't forget to "whoop" and discover the friendship that enfolds. Let me explain.

Laughter that is loud and spontaneous is what my family calls whooping. I am known for my noisy uncontrollable whoop, especially in social settings. People always want to know what's going on. Sometimes they start laughing. "Whoops" inspire talk, fun and quite a few laughs. They are exhilarating.

One of my sons routinely whoops with delight at the end of a three-mile run. He is exuberant, and all of our neighbors hear it! The sound of his yelp is an expression of pure joy from deep within. Along our short urban street, even in winter, he can be heard whooping two or three times outside our house and, if anyone is still listening, he'll whoop once again inside. Our neighbors give his now trademark "whoop" mixed reviews. To me, it is a joyous sound. I smile deeply whenever I hear it. I've noticed that when we go on vacation and he takes a long jog, the number of whoops spike. On one such morning, I happened to be on an early stroll myself. I counted fourteen whoops. A man stopped to listen, trying to figure out the source of this strange noise, as my son was no longer visible. This bystander was so puzzled that he tripped over a ledge to determine the origin and nature of this unexpected sound. To me, the unique whoop or laugh was a sound from the soul.

> **Humor has the power to uplift. Our mantra could be this simple: make people laugh.**

Try it yourself. Yelp or whoop. Really let loose a loud sound from deep within. Experience sheer exhilaration. To experience the family soul, we must be playful, even silly at times. Put your playfulness out there for all to see. Don't be afraid of letting the creative and silly emerge. Allow the lively, good-humored, lighthearted fool to come out and be a part of your day. Humor helps us get through the difficult times and handle struggle and stress. Bring humor into your daily life. And when you do, it will permeate into the life of your family. Humor has the power to uplift. Our mantra could be this simple: make people laugh.

✥

Laugh often, long and loud. Laugh until you gasp for breath. And if you have friends who make you laugh, spend lots and lots of time with them. Discover that when you make someone happy, it will make you become happy too.

Tool #2:
Re-create and Play Often

Recreation, or play, means to re-create. Ask yourself, "What do I do when I play? Does it strengthen my insides? Is the joy so great that I can experience the beauty of creating and recreating?" Play is neither business, nor obligation. It is not necessarily productive and not necessarily involved with something "worthwhile." There are times for these things, but they are not play. Play is pure joy. Play means to laugh, jump, celebrate and feel happy. If you don't look forward to your play, there is no joy in it. Think of a three-year-old skipping with infinite delight and you get the idea. Learning certain skills is not the purpose and end-goal of play, though many child development psychologists would argue that all play is learning.

When my youngest son was eight, he constantly reminded me of the meaning of pure play and the rare form of genuine joy that comes from it. He ran with delight. He screamed with enthusiasm at the plan to stay overnight at a friend's house. He raced to one end of the living room, slid, leaped up, ran back and slid again. His play brought undiluted joy. And the soul skipped.

Play can serve as a family antidote to stress. Most people will reply to the question "what do you do for fun?" by listing all the planned activities on their calendar. They go out to lunch with a friend, then to their daughter's soccer game, then to a play with friends. These activities are important, but they are not pure play

> **An empty calendar can bring such a feeling. It leaves the door open for your day to flow naturally, playfully.**

unless they bring a deep, spontaneous joy. (Note: An empty calendar can bring such a feeling. It leaves the door open for your day to flow naturally, playfully.)

Ways to Re-create—Physical, Creative and Zany Play

One family's preferred mode is rough, physical play: "We crawl around on the floor playing physically with our boys. And thank heaven they were boys, because they loved that gentle physical play, wrestling, pushing anything with wheels around, jumping on an old mattress we had in the basement, hitting a ball, playing soccer and riding ponies. The soul of our family was demonstrated by the number of holes in the good knees of our jeans."

Children are experts at play. They love to experiment and explore. Their brain, especially that of the pre-adolescent, is rich in theta waves. Theta waves occur in the earlier stages of sleep and are associated with states of enhanced imagination, daydreaming and sleep-dream activity. This is why a child's reality is full of bizarre, inventive, silly and fresh ideas. When theta waves are present, creativity is high. Sadly, adults are not as good at theta wave production anymore. But they can experience theta waves in their sleep, especially during dreamtime. Intriguingly, to connect with creative insights during a dream state, Thomas Edison slept straight up in an armchair. When he dozed off, an apparatus that he made using ball bearings and a pie plate would move to awaken him, at which time he would take note of any new or imaginative ideas.

While Edison's tactic is one way to tap into a creative state, play is much easier! Humor and joking around also make a person freer to explore and open up. Having fun disarms the inner censor, or a person's voice of judgment. If the operative rule is "anything goes" then all ideas, even the wild and wacky ones, can emerge. Research has found that teams of workers who laugh are more productive and creative. The message here is very clear for us all: Let loose and PLAY!

Family play can be "out there" in the zany zone. Every family, I'm sure, has a list of favorites. My own family has some favorites too. We built igloos in winter. We planted a vegetable garden together in spring. In the summertime, we loved to spend a lot of time on a hammock or reading under a tree. Our family has always has an annual summer frog race. We've discovered that when you blow gently on the frog's back end, it will leap. The only rule is that you can't pick up or touch the frog with your hands (or feet) at any point in the race. Every entrant (and frog) receives a prize at the finish line.

Cooking together can also be a form of play. It can be delightfully amusing and enjoyable. Never expect perfection. This would ruin the fun. It's best to expect that things will never turn out quite the same each time. If you have a recipe that must be followed to the finest detail, then don't select that one for your jointly prepared dish or meal. The fun is in the preparation, and this you can do together, everything from shopping for the ingredients, to chopping them up, to adding them to the pot, to watching them cook. Of course, eating the final dish brings great satisfaction, conversation and tasteful approval from all.

To get things going try these family fun play ideas: Dance with each other. Sing loudly together. Watch the sun set. Get up for the sunrise and then cook a big breakfast. Play baseball or basketball as a team, or break into several smaller teams that challenge one another. Play a wild game of cards with poker chips (or pennies). Everyone has to wear gambling visors. Go to an outdoor concert and take a picnic basket along. Don't forget to take a blanket. Plant a bush or tree and watch it grow. Be mischievous. Whether in the country or at the city zoo, moo at the cows and try to get them to "talk" back. Sometimes cows stare for a very long time, especially if you moo again. Sometimes I'll get a moo back. This only encourages me further.

Children Are Play Experts

Today's busy world can keep us from honoring the need to simply enjoy each other and focus on the present. Children can help you pay better attention. Being awake and present is an enormous gift. It's sort of like climbing high up on a tree and peering over the housetops to see the deep-blue ocean. A child would do this in a second.

Children naturally live their lives differently than adults. We need to hang out with them and relearn how to live in the present. Greater soulfulness occurs within the family when we do. Remember the scene in the movie "*Big*," where Tom Hanks, who was really a big kid in an adult tuxedo, eats the small pickled corncob as though it were a large ear of corn? Similarly, children often have a cookie-eating ritual of eating the outside first and saving the cream filled insides for the last bite. Children don't like to be rushed during these simple acts of pleasure. They want to taste the sweetness in every bite. They find great satisfaction in these kinds of everyday activities. They give honor to the simple joys of life.

> **Children don't like to be rushed during these simple acts of pleasure. They want to taste the sweetness in every bite. They find great satisfaction in these kinds of everyday activities. They give honor to the simple joys of life.**

We can turn to children to learn how to live enchantingly again. Children put a beautiful spin on the wonderment of life. The smallest thing can please or "feed" a child. It can be a drippy ice cream cone, a chocolate cupcake with colored sprinkles, planting a peach seed after eating the peach, climbing trees, throwing rocks in a pond or pennies in a fountain, a favorite walk, a wink, or the smell of something familiar cooking in the oven. These pleasures feed their happiness, and their souls, and yours too. Yes, adults can also squeal with joy, laugh deeply and express delight as children do so well. Watch closely. Discover how children enjoy life as it is, without demanding that it be any different. Children can show us how to experience time to its fullest and live abundantly in the present.

Adults waste a lot of time thinking about what they did in the past and what they have left to do in the future. This focus causes stress and anxiety. Because children quite naturally focus on what they are doing in the present, they can teach us how to reduce our stress and relax. By giving a task or activity our complete attention and focus, we experience the present. Children can become so completely involved in what they are doing that they don't want to leave it. We can often intercept them thinking about their present experience or something related to it. Adults call this daydreaming! How often do we find them in this "pause phase" and tell them to hurry up? Living in the moment is their chosen path.

There are other lessons that we can learn from how children relate to time. They don't like interruptions of any kind. They prefer time that is totally focused on an activity. They love to eat and talk for the taste or joy of it. They especially like the down time of naps, although they may not admit it! They want time for themselves whenever possible, and search for it with passion!

You will also find that children are quite open to talking about a variety of topics and love to poke about conversationally. If you give them more control over their own room, they enjoy playing there and like making it more attractive, whether it be lining up their toys, organizing their puzzles, or putting their own artwork on their walls. They find great comfort and satisfaction in their efforts to creatively enhance their space.

Appropriately, children don't give you much time to work on vacation! If they do, then it's a clear indication that you aren't taking a vacation. They seem to have a better handle on these longer play periods than adults. They *really* play. They play so hard that they like to come home and take time to reflect on that play before going back to a routine. They remind us that it is best not to rush into the old routine after these longer rest periods. They tell us that we should plan occasional days off to play again—soon.

Be sure your family engages in physical, creative and unconventional play. Let children show you the joy of living in the present. Tap into their expertise, as they put a playful spin on the wonderment of life.

13. "E" for Emotion—Elevate and Celebrate Emotion and Find Ways to Evoke It

"Once I walked into our ten-year-old son's bedroom when he was listening to his stereo. I found a disco tape, put it in and cranked the music up. We both danced and laughed in his little room for most of the evening, stopping every now and then to take a breath and to talk about nothing in particular. We chatted about different objects in his room, laughed at each other's dancing, and he began to open up about some things he was thinking and feeling, disco music blaring all the while. It was a great bonding time for us and just before I left his room he said: 'This was the best night of my life.'"

—Interviewed parent

The emotion of merriment, described by this parent, is contagious. Listen to another person describe her merry time. It is pure bliss. "When I am with my sisters, completely letting loose, just being silly together and ourselves, these are some of my happiest times. It's sheer, unadulterated fun where we can be ourselves and just enjoy each other's company. It is the best, most relaxed, most enjoyable feeling."

But these sisters also experience emotionally weary times together, grappling with difficulty, individually or together. "While we may be saddened by an event, we bring each other up with our presence and by being there to go through the hardship together. It is these times, either supercharged with happiness, or in a valley of despair, that I feel most connected with my sisters. It's a feeling of pure, raw emotion—and us bonding as we experience those emotions together."

The Emotion of Merriment

Happy energy is powerful. One must yell out to express it. "Let's be merry!" or "Let's party!" Picture all family members clicking their heels up in the air, simultaneously, and you get the idea. Hidden within the word, "enjoyment" is the word "joy." There can be a lot of joy when family members come together, do fun things and share ideas with one another. During these happy or merry times, the soul comes out to play. How do families reach this place of joy and what does it look and feel like? Advises one parent: "I don't think it can be forced. It just happens sometimes when you least expect it. It feels like we are finding it more frequently, now that our children are more comfortable in their own skins. It doesn't happen when there is insecurity or competition."

Let's listen to two different families, as they share how they discovered the parameters of this sought-after joy. Begins one parent, "We find joy at weddings, graduations, birthdays and holidays. We've planned and communicated with each other for the event. Then the time together results in lots of smiling, talking, laughing, looking at each other, hugging, touching in affection and kidding. It is a time free of pain, anger, hurt, hate. The people have come with the desire and purpose of having fun and loving—they have let the struggles go for that period of time."

A second family member talked about her merry family times: "Our family is super happy together when we are all engaged in an activity that we all enjoy, like being outdoors, cycling, walking, playing tennis, debating an issue, playing a board game, building something,

> **"The people have come with the desire and purpose of having fun and loving—they have let the struggles go for that period of time."**

writing something, creating something, having dinner around the table. This is a place where we can relax and be ourselves and listen to each other. It doesn't happen if life gets in the way, we get over-committed and we don't make time and space for each other, find quiet time and reconnect with each other."

Celebrating Together

Celebration is an act of the soul. How does your family celebrate together, in small, informal ways as well as large celebrations? One parent explains: "Birthdays and holidays have always been important family celebrations for us. I am big on traditions. For instance, we have a Christmas cookie-decorating contest every year and we all vote on the best cookie, which is not always the prettiest but certainly the most creative. Getting there is most of the fun." She adds: "We also have certain traditions on Christmas Eve and Day that center around friends, family and togetherness. We go to lots of holiday celebrations outside the house, like a Christmas carol sing along. We take another family with us every year and all sit together and sing holiday songs, then we all go out for a special dinner."

Continuing, she adds: "Easter is the same, dressing up and going out to brunch with other families, decorating and hiding eggs in the yard. One New Year's Eve I gave everyone a roll of aluminum foil and we each made funny hats and took pictures of each other. I still have those hats. In fact, funny hats have played a role in many of our holiday celebrations. We have reindeer ears, bunny ears and Santa hats, just to be silly, and even hats for our poor dog, who hates them and refuses to move if you put one on him! Little celebrations are important too, a special ice cream cake with a 'Way To Go!' on it when our child has accomplished something or received an award."

Reflecting on her family dynamics, another person says: "We are super happy when we are all together as a family and healthy. We weren't as happy when we lived in different states. We truly missed the sharing. Celebrations weren't the same until we were all together again. Humor is always at the core of our family. We could be our own reality show. We entertain one another even today. I think we are all stand-up comedians. Even though my mother can't remember or recall short-term things as much as she used to, her sense of humor is very much intact."

The Merry and the Weary Dance

Joyfulness and weariness live side-by-side. One's joy is felt by others. And the same is true with weariness; it too is passed forward. We can learn to gain strength from each other in both the merry and the weary periods. Like merriment, then, weariness is part of the soul. A family member may be suffering, eclipsing the family's sense of joy. If we are lucky, weariness lurks in the cupboard for a short time. One family was nearly always merry even though they experienced some in-and-out weariness, as a family member describes here: "The weary has been the deaths and illnesses that our family has endured. Also, because divorces took place when we were young children, we were a smaller immediate family of women most of the time. My mom was divorced from my sister's father at a young age, and divorced twice from my father when I was little, but she had primary custody of us. And when my mom remarried again, my stepfather and my father were both very present in our lives. But, because these marriages didn't last very long, we were usually an immediate family of women."

Weary dances in and out. Hopefully, the merry times lead and twirl and guide. But when the weary dominates, know the merry can return.

Weary dances in and out. Hopefully, the merry times lead and twirl and guide. But when the weary dominates, know the merry can return.

Four Ways to Find Merriment

When does the merry predictably occur? While there can be no limits to the origins of merriment, four "conditions" surfaced above others in my interviews. First and to no surprise, family vacations are a key source of merriment! Shares one family spokesperson, "we are super happy when we leave on a trip together, relaxing on a beach, eating together. We have worked really hard, individually and as a family, to get to the point that we can take a break and be together and do things together. Physically and emotionally, everybody feels great, although we may need to catch up on some sleep. At the end of the vacation sometimes we don't want to go back to our 'real' world of responsibilities."

Second, like vacations, celebrations of all types, whether a birthday, holiday, or special occasion, bring merriment. Family members make the day special. They may go out to dinner, have a cake and open gifts, or cook a special meal. The gatherings can be large and exuberant or quiet and intimate. Reflects one interviewee, "My mom has eight brothers and sisters with a total of 25 grandchildren. We would have monthly family gatherings growing up. This was a big source of happiness from my childhood. We still try to get together for large events, but it's hard as we are all growing up and moving to different cities."

Third, merriment happens when members just relax and have fun. Here are some conditions, as described by one family member: "We are content together when no one is trying to control, when we can relax and just get absorbed in something like a board game or bowling. My oldest daughter loves to come up with family activities – we went to the State Fair last year. Every Christmas we drive out to the suburbs and look at the holiday lights in our sweats with hot chocolate in the car." She continued: "We all love going to my sister's house in another nearby state – we just relax and have fun. My husband brings his guitar and plays with my sister's husband for hours. We just relaxed there. I have a dear friend from college and when she and her husband come over we all just sit around and have fun and laugh."

A fourth way to guarantee merriment: cut back on media, like phones and TV. Instead, do tech opposites: get out in nature, talk deeply and share ideas, or play a sport. The possibilities are endless, if you think creatively and playfully. Shares one tech-exhausted parent: "Technology can make a family weary. It's disturbing how much time is wasted 'living' on cell phones, texting and Internet surfing. I'll walk into a room and the two adult children and my husband are all playing with their phones instead of interacting with each other."

One mother shares her strategy: "I think of shielding. We never watch television as a family much. My husband and I never watch television, and our kids watch it very little (except Mr. Rogers and Sesame Street when they were young), but we are more about books and reading and being outside. We just love to be together on vacation over the summer, and we traditionally eat together, ski together, weddings – those all would be happy times."

The weary can pick up again, offsetting the family dynamic. Family members can get exhausted and irritable from too much work—office, school and household maintenance. An overly tired parent cannot think straight, creating a divide, especially if children have boundless energy. Or, an overly tired child can act out, creating frustration for all. Exhaustion is often overlooked as a cause of family tension. Parents and children and friends all may miss its impact on the family dynamic, until they experience an "ah-hah moment" realizing that he or she is simply tired. More

Creative, Happy Times Generated by One Family

One veteran grandmother shared a powerfully happy time that her entire family shared each summer. It was a one-day barbeque cook-off contest in Wisconsin. A gargantuan event, food and equipment were brought in (semi-trucks, mind you), prepared (and eaten!), and certified judges awarded substantial prize money. Her daughter and son-in-law were annual contestants—with all the other family members cheering them on. Further, she described more happy times when her family took a trip to visit old friends from their time living in Grand Rapids. Their families had children with almost identical ages and they had a remarkable time together. One of the friend's adult children lived on the river. It was a very happy time for all—complete with tubing, eating, playing games and having campfires.

This same family had big reunions with her mother and her mother's siblings every four years. They missed it this last four-year cycle, as her mother, who planned it every year, passed away. Her mother's family would also have a mini one, the two years in between. So every two years, they would have some type of reunion. They often found a place where they had a big meeting area or great room, and a swimming pool. Picture their happy souls connecting and you can almost experience it yourself. Their emotion is contagious.

times than not, fatigue can explain each and every "strange" behavior exhibited between family members and friends. When we get overtired, the weary comes out to play. Joyful energy recedes. But, luckily, we may just need a nap!

Here's my point: The "merry" does a continual dance with the "weary." Become aware of this continual back-and-forth swing, and come to terms with the wearying challenge, embracing both the joys and sadnesses of family life.

❧❧

Happy energy is powerful. Celebration is an act of the soul. Every family possesses the ability to find merriment. Consider vacations, trips, special celebratory days, holiday gatherings, reunions and game playing—and don't forget to pull the plug on the tech equipment.

Tool #3: Speak from the Heart

Speaking from the heart means expressing warmth, sharing thoughts and feelings, having compassion for others, and generating feelings of connectedness. If a person's behavior needs to be corrected, the heartfelt parent or friend will talk with gentle, helpful, kind, truthful, sensitive and well-timed words. This person knows that hurts are toxic and have no place in growth and relationship building. Communicating emotion and speaking from the heart bring profound and fundamental change. It "awakens" a child, or relative or friend. As Carl Jung so eloquently states: "Your vision will become clear only when you look into your heart. Who looks outside, dreams. Who looks within, awakens."

Teaching "heart work," or how to express what is in your heart, should be part of the "work" of family members and friends alike. Let's face it. Some of us are better at it than others. Quite often, grandparents are particularly adept at expressing emotion. Sometimes aunts and uncles display emotional acumen and can shine on this front, just when needed. Often, in-laws are superb at heart talking too. If you have an emotionally gifted "star" within your family or circle of friends, then use this person to serve as a teacher.

Five Kinds of Emotional Intelligence

Daniel Goleman in his book *Emotional Intelligence: Why It Can Matter More Than I.Q.* discusses *five* aspects of emotional insight. Each is critical. Each is powerful. And each can be learned by children and adults alike. The first is self-awareness, or the ability to express what one feels and why. It means being able to say "this feels right" and know why it does. This type of knowledge simplifies personal decision-making. Families are ideally set up to assume the task of teaching this aspect of emotional intelligence. Nurture self-awareness on your family front. How? Encourage "Who Am I?" activities and "Star Quality" discussions like those discussed in the next chapter (#14). Come up with your own ideas. Be creative. You will be surprised how much fun it is to explore your "self" and share what you have learned with others.

A second feature of emotional intelligence Goleman identifies is being able to manage emotions and feelings, especially the feelings of anxiety, anger and sadness. Left unmanaged, these feelings colonize the frontal lobe, shrinking the ability to learn and posing a threat to others in and outside the home.

Optimism and hope, a third type of emotional intelligence, can also be learned. According to Goleman, targeted programs exist that help teach these qualities. I strongly believe that families are the best place to teach them! Fortunately, my own mom's optimism or "glass half full" approach to life was taught and passed along to her three children. On her 100th birthday, my brother Paul acknowledged it in his speech, and then articulated how he too had passed it along to his own three daughters through her example. Again, families are ideally positioned to take on the critically vital task of nurturing optimism and hope. We need these qualities to survive.

A fourth feature of emotional intelligence is having social skills or the ability to tend to the emotions of others. Significant to our discussion, most all emotions are universal and contagious. People give social cues to one another and these cues can be read. I worry about the lack of social skills when technology dominates the scene. Just think of tablets, iPhones, computers, iTunes, instead of watching others and learning what their social cues communicate, and you get the gist of my worry. Families can set up rituals to cut back on the techy equipment, and encourage more talk and participation.

There is another key feature of emotional intelligence. It is empathy or discovering and knowing how people feel. It means expressing compassion and caring. Bullies, for example, have not learned empathy and pounce on their prey because of it. Let's zoom in on the work of empathy, as it is especially helpful to our soul work. All people can learn to read feelings. Master this early on—the sooner, the better. Put yourself in the other person's shoes. See that your younger child is upset and worried because the book is too difficult to read. See that your adult child is sad because their friend didn't get accepted into the program. See that your friend is still grieving because his mother, who died six months ago, is still deeply missed.

Feelings reflect reality. They emerge from inside the person and become invaluable information. To honor a person's feelings is to understand and strengthen that person. Sometimes, all a person needs to know is that someone else is aware of how he or she feels and why. Acknowledging feelings—expressing empathy—may be all that is necessary to fix a hurt or rectify a bad situation.

Though well meaning, attempts to "cheer up" others often fall flat. We often deny, dismiss and ignore the feelings of others, or worse—try to talk the person out of having this feeling. Alternatively, we can validate a person's feeling—you may be surprised to learn that is all he or she needed. Take a close look at the words you use when your children and friends share their feelings. Effective responses express openness and acceptance. Learn to read the child or friend and respond with candidness. Empathy is critical in weaving closeness between family members. Learning to speak from the heart is one of our most important lessons. Make emotional expression contagious and ongoing within your family. The soul thrives on it.

What is Compassion?

Compassion is having a concern for the well-being of others. The word itself is from the Latin *cum patior*, to suffer with. Compassion means understanding another person to such a degree that you can empathize with their feelings and thoughts. Compassion inspires kindness, generosity and inclusiveness among family members.

Compassion means being in the heart of another person. The closer we are, the more we can feel or relate to others' situations—to be in their hearts and to experience their emotions, whether they harbor happiness, confusion, sorrow, pain or misery. Genuine compassion results in feeling concerned and responsible for another. It is not enough just to feel it; one must do something with it.

Compassionate relationships pull others in by listening and asking questions, making others feel safe to speak honestly. A compassionate person cares and encourages and helps others. A compassionate person can answer "yes" to: "Did I make him feel better about himself? Did I make her feel like she was capable of discovering and achieving more than she thought she could?" Compassion adds texture to relationships. The bond deepens. Compassion nourishes the soul.

Manifesting Compassion

Compassion can be as simple as saying a kind word to another person. It means sitting down to talk with someone and personally explaining a difficult problem or situation. Or compassion can also be expressed on a greater scale, like setting up a foundation to serve those in need or raising money for an environmental cause. When there is a burning desire to affect change on a larger scale, it can be powerful for the recipients as well as those who are doing the giving.

According to the Dalai Lama in his book *An Open Heart: Practicing Compassion in Everyday Life*, true compassion "has the intensity and spontaneity of a loving mother caring for her suffering baby. Throughout the day, such a mother's concern for her child affects all her thoughts and actions. This is the attitude we are working to cultivate with each and every being. When we experience this, we have generated great compassion." Families can work to cultivate compassion. Caring for a needy group without food or housing, and other kinds of "larger" compassionate acts, is nurturing, like that of a loving mother.

The act of compassion (it's not just a thought) can be expressed individually in small ways, leaving the world a little better for our having passed through it. There are ways to generate compassion right in one's home by how one acts and talks. You don't have to invent a new polio vaccine. Discover the phenomenal power of small expressions of compassion. If one can make a difference in the lives of family members—no matter how small—that person really will have accomplished something. There is a cumulative impact of individual acts of compassion on the individual and the family.

Why Engage In Compassion?

No matter how microscopic, acts of compassion are of great consequence. Families that nurture compassion among members often find it to be a constant source of renewal. For example, small acts of compassion—

as simple as patting someone on the shoulder, preparing a home-cooked meal for a sick member, or easing someone's pain who is going through a crisis – all make a huge difference to a family member or friend. Whether you are on the giving or receiving end, such acts of compassion make you feel that others truly care and are there to help out. It's up to parents and other family members to encourage compassionate understanding and acts of caring behavior. When other family members see that the family culture encourages and nurtures compassion, it brings everyone closer together.

The Road to Compassion— "Other-discovery, Not Self-discovery"

One of my favorite books on compassion is *Field Notes on the Compassionate Life: A Search for the Soul of Kindness*. The author, Marc Ian Barasch, says that the road to a compassionate life occurs through "other-discovery" rather than "self-discovery". He quotes Father Thomas Keating, a Benedictine monk, who said, "The American Way is to first feel good about you, and then feel good about others. But spiritual traditions say it's really the other way around – that you develop a sense of goodness by giving of yourself."

Don't wait until your "self" is mature, developed and happy to show compassion for others. Do it now, because the focus on giving to others leads to feeling good yourself.

It should be no surprise, then, that acts of compassion are a poignant and powerful web that unites one another in the family. Encourage family members to express compassion. Teach them to leave a legacy of giving; make kindness a part of their lives; and use their personal gifts to do as much as they can for others. This is how fami-

Encourage family members to express compassion. Teach them to leave a legacy of giving; make kindness a part of their lives; and use their personal gifts to do as much as they can for others. This is how families and schools and communities, and even the world, is transformed.

lies and schools and workplaces and communities, and even the world, is transformed.

A close friend gave me a tiny paper hand-painted box some time ago. When you remove its colorful oval top, there is a three-dimensional glimmering paper gold heart inside. The heart is beautifully cut so that it appears thick and three-dimensional. In the middle of the heart sets a large eye that immediately pops out. Wings extend out from each side of the heart, as though the heart can fly. In the sky, which is the background inside the box, sits a huge bright sparkling star. Rays of sunlight circle the heart. The visual message is powerful: *Those who see with the heart have wings to fly to the stars.* This sums it up. Heart work is essential for families. Every person can learn to speak from the heart and tap into an awesome source of compassion and love.

Heart in a Box.

Find an emotionally gifted star within your family and use this person to teach "heartwork." It is simply that important for children, teens and adults to learn to express their feelings, speak from their hearts and master the lessons of emotional intelligence. Empathize or put yourself in the other person's shoes. Compassionate words and actions make an enormous difference.

14. "A" for Acceptance— Accept All Family Members and Create a Safe Haven

"Treat each other as individuals, as equals, as complex stories to be heard."

—Unknown

"I am convinced that the crucial factor in what happens both *inside* people and *between* people is the picture of individual worth that each person carries around with him—his pot."

—Virgina Satir in *Peoplemaking*

Can each of your family members say aloud "I accept myself" or "I love myself"? When they have self-acceptance, each can yell out "I like myself just the way I am!" Too many children and teens are brought up never to accept or like themselves. Self-acceptance—embracing, getting in touch with, and enjoying being oneself—is vital to every individual's personal development and ability to find fulfillment in life and give their best to others. It says to take a gentle look at yourself and honestly enjoy and appreciate who you are. Rather than be tough and critical, it says to be easy, kind and gentle. Uniqueness lends value. Differences are awesome. Help your children, teens, spouse and friends to think this way and to honor their self—without changing anything. She or he doesn't need to be thinner, smarter, faster, older, or more attractive. These "improvements" can be tossed out with the moldy bread. There isn't a perfect way to live a life. It's only perfect if it's right for you.

There is only one way to learn acceptance. It starts with first understanding differences. By appreciating why and how someone is different and how we ourselves are unique, acceptance will grow in your heart.

This is not always easy. A wise grandmother illuminated the difficulties. Listen in on her insightful perspective: "Yes, family can be a safe place. But safety in the family is precarious; it comes and goes. Safety depends on trust, which depends on honesty. People are flawed, make mistakes and get lost. People think differently. Our life experiences are different, and that adds up to a lot of differences! It is ever-changing and unpredictable. This means that some families might be a safe place for all members, some, or none." She concluded, and I concur, "it depends on the individual in the family and how aware and guided they are" to find a safe place for growth.

Fight Against Self-criticism

Each person has unique qualities—voice, personality, looks, interests—and these give distinction. We can learn to love each other and ourselves as we are, inadequacies and all. And we can encourage each other to take a close look at our essential "self," what exists inside and outside. We can nurture a great love for our individual qualities and learn to refuse to compromise who we are. Parents can help children and teens discover this powerful life lesson: Other people can't make you feel inferior, unless you give them your consent. These are essential strategies for anyone. But accepting the self unconditionally is especially important for children and teens, when personalities, feelings, or values are undergoing major shifts. Spouses and friends can always use a boost of self-acceptance too.

Because life is an internal journey, fighting against self-criticism can be a solitary pursuit. Each person must discover that she or he is blissfully magnificent. Each life has a drum beat all its own. The bumps in the road, rather than the smooth stretches, are what make the trip dynamic and colorful. So, don't try to change your child or teen. Encourage each to become a unique individual within. Love each child and teen and person, just as he or she is, with all your heart. Acceptance is what a person needs now.

Listen to Your Inner Voice

As a new voice emerges from your child or teen, learn to appreciate its tenor, whether playful or grave, forceful or hesitant, monotone or melodious, brazen or nervous, resonant or shrill. Its uniqueness gives it force and power. Your child or teen is becoming a star and learning how to sparkle. Let her know that you love how she expresses herself. With its inflections and interruptions, her voice is emerging—glorious, spectacular and unique. Encourage her full self-expression. Help her see her power, as best you can. And finally, believe in her as she endures difficulties and travels courageously along to reach her final destination—truly awakened with self-acceptance and a sense of her dignity and self worth. Accept and celebrate your child or teen's emerging individuality.

Family is a place where acceptance and encouragement begin. But just like any situation, it is easy for family to judge as well. One mature almost-thirty woman shared this relevant story: "Because each family member has their own beliefs, personality and the way they think things should be, they bring this to the table and have a perspective on your life. This is a hurdle but it is surmountable. In college my sister began telling me that she didn't approve of some of the things I did or decisions I made. I sat her down and brought to her attention that she was holding her standards and values over my head, and that I wouldn't go to her as my confidant if I felt

> **As a new voice emerges from your child or teen, learn to appreciate its tenor, whether playful or grave, forceful or hesitant, monotone or melodious, brazen or nervous, resonant or shrill. Its uniqueness gives it force and power. Your child or teen is becoming a star and learning how to sparkle.**

judged." She continued: "She agreed that it isn't her job as my sister to make judgments over how I lived my life. After that we agreed that she could tell me her opinion, because I know she does have my best interest at heart, but that it is my prerogative to disagree and not feel judged if I did otherwise. And ever since then I haven't had a hard time coming to her about anything." Her sister learned to accept her emerging new individuality.

Accept Yourself, First!

In addition to acceptance by other family members, accepting the self unconditionally is important at every point in life. Here is a major revelation that a mother shared with me regarding her son's path to self-acceptance. Her son told her that he was gay. He talked about the role that "self acceptance" played in his own ability to embrace his sexuality. He explained that keeping this a secret left an overwhelming feeling of exhaustion. Now open and honest with himself, and "out," he was no longer tired, plus he got rid of a sick feeling knowing that sharing of his sexuality was still forthcoming.

Here's what is important to keep in mind. He expressed who he is. He accepted himself. No longer does he carry the weight of this secret on his back. He was burdened by this secret for a very long time. He has now accepted himself as a gay man on the road to finding himself. He has inhered many other qualities in addition to the newly shared orientation.

There is a natural tendency towards privacy, and even secrecy, in teens and young adults who are exploring, finding and understanding their feelings. If you think back to your own teen years, it takes quite a while to explore and answer the question of "Who am I?" Our culture often ostracizes certain groups and is not readily supportive of this personal discovery. Yet honoring the self requires a circulation of freedom, reverence, self-realization, trust and courage. When it is accomplished, one is awakened with self-acceptance and a sense of dignity and self-worth.

Try Not to Judge

"I'm stupid because I don't have a girlfriend." "I'm not a good writer because I'm just not creative." "I suck in acting class." "I stink at soccer because I can't trap the ball." "I am not doing well at my new job because I don't have the right computer skills." All of these self-demeaning thoughts originate from an intruder we might call "the Judge." He is the inner critic, the mastermind of negative feelings and low self-esteem. While the Judge lives inside everyone, he especially likes to take charge during times of massive change.

How can the Judge be so effective? He uses a strategy called "partial validity." Here is how it works: After missing a shot, the Judge says to the player, "You suck at basketball." This is partially true because he did miss a shot (even though everybody misses some shots), but now the player thinks he's terrible at basketball. Masterfully, the Judge always backs up the insults with partially true facts. Most of the time, these facts are insignificant—like missing a goal, doing poorly on one area of a test, or bombing on a speech.

Stealth is a critical part of his strategy. To most everyone, the Judge's involvement in their lives is imperceptible. Whispering slyly within their minds, he criticizes every move and turn. The Judge especially likes to pop up and be critical when a person is involved in something important—like going out on a big date, making a difficult speech to a professional group, or racing against a fast jogger in a 5K race.

Dr. John Cooper, a clinical psychologist for almost forty years, was an expert on the Judge. A gifted therapist with a wonderful practical side, he could cut through personal chaos. (I know this for a fact!) Before his untimely heart attack, he shared with me his insights on how the Judge maneuvers inside our heads. According to Dr. Cooper, the Judge is especially active when a person has feelings of confusion, isolation, embarrassment, or loss of control—times when one is barely hanging on to their insides. Stress builds up and control wanes, setting a person up for internal self-indictments and criticisms. An avalanche of anxiety manifests, interfering with our daily lives and even our sleep at night. Unfortunately, internal chaos subsides and confusion, self-doubt and anxiety run rampant in the person's psyche.

The Judge

The Judge is sneaky and clever at his craft, taking full advantage of inner turmoil and vulnerability.

What is the best way to counteract the Judge? First, stay alert to his sneaky strategy—which is to harbor partially valid evidence against your "self" and put a negative spin on your worth and potential. You might also try using a "Judge Book" to catch the Judge in the act. This technique helps disprove the Judge's insults and prevents him from playing such a major role in shaping your self-image. Get a blank notebook. When you feel bad or uncomfortable about yourself, explore why you have this feeling. Try to expose the Judge's accusations (e.g., "you suck at dancing") and write them down. Give it time to simmer, and then go back after a day. Put on your Detective hat and search for the pieces to the puzzle—break down each one of the Judge's insults, dissect their partial truth, and observe their irrational and inaccurate nature.

To sum up: when you are going through life transitions or exploring new horizons and territories, the resulting chaos provides the Judge fertile ground in which to plant accusations and self-demeaning thoughts. When you feel bad about yourself, know that the Judge may be sitting high on your shoulders. Confront the internal Judge head-on, and help other family members do so too.

Create A Safe Haven for Your Family

Family serves as a refuge for learning self-acceptance. How can individual family members support another member who is learning to accept the self? One interviewed parent nailed it. He emphatically stressed how important it is to never judge and never stop loving each person, as well as to engage in selfless listening: "Acceptance of each individual is *so* important and sometimes hard, especially when a family member seems to be going in the wrong direction. If love is the basis of the relationships and everyone knows it, then harmony will occur, but maybe not immediately. Learning to put self aside for humble listening is the key."

In order for acceptance of self and others to occur, one needs a feeling of support, safety and security. When these exist, the family can be a supportive and encouraging place where members are out of harm's way. They reach out, embrace, comfort and awaken each other's powers, and welcome everyone just the way they are—tears, fears, struggles, hardships and all.

Family provides a safe haven for each member. Three interviewees persuasively shared their thoughts on this topic. The first described her family "safe haven" or sanctuary as the faith they shared: "It is not always easy to see someone in pain or struggling, and feel like you can't help them. But again, the soul of our family is faith. I've watched us go through the worst of times where it didn't seem like it was going to change. I watched my mother or grandmother pray and hold on to their beliefs that it would change. They would always say, 'Prayer changes things, you have to step out on faith.'" She continued: "Growing up, when anyone would ask my grandmother, 'how are you doing today?' she would reply, 'I'm kicking, but not high, flopping, but can't fly, I'm weak, but I'm willing.' It is now in our immediate family's DNA to keep going and be willing to push through the hardships. It doesn't mean that everything is going to be the way we want it to be; but, as a family we can endure whatever the situation is because we have one another to lean on."

Family becomes a safe haven for self-exploration and acceptance of each other. One mother shared the nuances of how this is played out in her family: "My husband and I worked very hard to be successful in our careers and we do put a lot of pressure on the girls and sometimes our first reaction is more critical, but we do have very open discussions and are honest about our expectations. My oldest daughter is most afraid of disappointing me, which I find interesting because I tell her all the time how proud I am of her and how she has now become my role model. She and I are so close and have such heart-to-heart talks all the time, but if she has what she thinks is a major issue, she will first approach my husband and get his reaction." She stresses these intricacies: "We all support each other very well as a family but I don't think I am initially good at allowing the girls to be who they are. I have a tendency to second guess or try and get them to see things my way, but eventually will come around. We try and encourage our girls not to lock themselves down into one thing and try and experiment and do different things. My older daughter especially finds comfort in focusing and staying on point and although I admire her tenacity, I encourage her to feel uncomfortable because it opens you up to aspects of life you didn't consider." Life is challenging and we are imperfect and family can be a safe place to turn when we are searching for answers or solutions.

Consider a third perspective on family as a "safe haven." There is a bit of history to this one. My interviewee had just heard three men speak on a panel on Martin Luther King Day about an eight-track audiotape they had made fifty years ago. The tape had sat in a shoebox and was played for the first time to the audience, including the three men, who had graduated from college in 1963. All three had gone down to Alabama and Mississippi to register people to vote. This unheard tape was about their personal experiences while in the Deep South fighting the racial divide. Two of them were arrested multiple times. All were in danger of losing their lives; one was beaten severely. Now a minister, a counselor and the other a journalist, the men strongly felt that freedom of information and truth in speaking were the key messages to their experience. They sought a "save haven." During the panel discussion, all three credited their mothers for being strong influences in their lives and serving as a compass—not directing, not necessarily pointing the way—but setting an example and letting them follow their own path. Each man on the panel said he had experienced family as a safe place to accept, grow and awaken his powers.

In each of these three examples the family offers a homebase to share faith, to experiment and to discover an internal compass—along the arduous road to self-discovery. Families that engage in teaching members to accept their self accomplish this powerful work by welcoming members just the way they are, by offering support and encouragement, and by extending a hand to ensure each member is headed down the right path.

ॐ

Each person has unique qualities—and these traits create diversity. Accept all family members, regardless of differences. Learn to love them just as they are. Accept yourself unconditionally. Fight against self-criticism, listen to your inner voice and try not to judge. Family can serve as a refuge or safe haven for learning self-acceptance.

Tool #4:
Nurture Equality and Appreciate Differences

Care for each individual within the family. Discover the strengths of each member, nurture equality and appreciate that each individual is gifted in varied and magical ways.

Discovering Each Other's Strengths

Picture a magnificent star shining down from the sky on a clear summer night. It's you. What makes you a star? We all have what I call "Star Quality." As you look more closely at the star, you can see distinct rays of light shooting from it. What do you beam out to others? What makes you unique? What qualities do you display in your closest relationships? Describe three of your beams of light, that is, the three qualities that are your strong suits—what makes you unique. I have listed mine below:

My beams of light:

1. Listening deeply

2. Teaching

3. Kindness

Now draw a picture of a large star on a piece of paper. Write in your three star qualities. Pin the star on you and wear it. Are your qualities more visible now? You need to see them more clearly. Know you are a star. Do the same for your children. Draw a blank star for each child, and write three qualities on it.

Star qualities focus on the question "Who am I?" We answer it with words or phrases that identify what we express to others. Rewrite them below, as the strengths that best describe you personally.

WHO AM I?

List three strengths you see in yourself:

1. _____

2. _____

3. _____

Next, do some more deep-down thinking and complete the question below, asking youself to identify your personal needs.

WHAT IS IMPORTANT TO ME?

List three needs you see in yourself:

1. _____

2. _____

3. _____

After you have completed this focus on your own strengths and needs, pick another family member (parents and extended family members are included too) and shift to getting to know theirs. Note those characteristics below that you feel best describe their strengths and needs. Have them do the same for you.

WHO ARE YOU?

List three strengths you see in another family member:

1. _____

2. _____

3. _____

WHAT IS IMPORTANT TO YOU?

List three needs you see in another family member:

1. _____

2. _____

3. _____

When you both have completed the description of each other, share this information. How accurate is your description of the other's strengths and needs, compared to their own description? Do the characteristics match? In some cases, they may be very close. In others, they may be quite different. Why? We may not spend enough time or express enough interest in other family members. Or there may be too much focus placed on one individual at the sacrifice of another's needs. Or some individuals may try to hide their more personal characteristics. Some parents try to impose their own strengths and needs onto their child, instead of seeing what the child "beams" into the family setting.

Here's the key point: Get to know the strengths and needs of each family member. As parents, we must look closely to see the strengths and needs in our children, then help them to see their unique strengths for themselves. In a strong family, children and parents alike will show their strengths and express their needs. They will grow and develop individually and nourish one another. Knowing who I am and what my needs are and who you are and what your needs are can help us choose activities for personal growth and fun. What do you want to learn, acquire and achieve? How can you find ways to satisfy your personal needs? What can parents do to facilitate this personal growth? And what can siblings do to help one another? Family members can help each individual find the right path to personal growth by matching every strength and need with at least one activity or action. As family members, we must learn to do some things for ourselves, and some things for others in the family. Parents can encourage their children to have this double focus. *Discover your family stars.*

Nurture Equality

One essential value that can be shared by all families is an appreciation of each individual. Accepting our differences and celebrating the power of each person can, and should, be a pervasive value within a family. Recognizing individuals—as they are and who they are—is the soulful work of family. Everyone can learn to see the unique qualities of others, and have an openness and nonjudgmental view toward differences in family members. Each family member has different gifts. When the expression of a diverse range of gifts is encouraged, then each person will grow and flourish. Parents, grandparents and all family members can be promoters of equality and diversity.

Alarmingly, most families tend to be patriarchal and hierarchical. They end up having unequal participants—the mother and father may be authoritarian in their parenting. They may use their power to pressure, demand, punish, coerce, impose and dominate. I believe that families should be more democratic. Rudolf Dreikurs, M.D. in his book *Children: The Challenge* provides a list of characteristics for both democratic and autocratic families.

The soul is freer to do its dance in democratic families. These families, stresses Dreikurs, have a knowledgeable leader who recommends that the entire group take action when it is necessary. There is no authority figure who says, "You do it because I said you have to." This power and pressure would be inappropriate and ineffective. It dominates and imposes the demands of one over the other. Instead, the parent listens and respects the other family members, encourages independence and offers guidance in the spirit of cooperation. Rather than punishment, there are logical consequences that "teach" – a person is allowed to experience the consequences of his or her actions, providing an honest and real-world learning situation. Encouragement is given to create a sense of accomplishment and self-respect. Then everyone can participate and help out, because the journey together is an arduous one.

Families can endure hardships of all kinds. Their goal is to be able to handle the disheartening and challenging ups and downs that happen along the way. When families nurture the value of equality, each person feels important. Each person feels their significance within the family. This does not assume that all members have the same skills or equal "gifts." It means that each person in the family has unique talents that contribute to the group.

Appreciate and Respect Differences

Each person's intelligence is unique and useful in different ways. And there is a magical quality to the study of intelligence, if we broaden our definition. An IQ score measures intelligence with words and numbers. It provides a traditional definition of ability. It says a child is smart if she can read a story and understand what happened, or do advanced math calculations with ease. SAT scores reflect these more traditional types of intelligence, but such tests actually restrict the definition of intelligence.

Ask yourself if you think of these people as intelligent: The mechanic who quickly identified why your car wouldn't run, the little girl next door who wrote a moving poem about how much she liked your grandmother, the friend who can understand why you feel the way you do before you share your thoughts, the young band member who can play four instruments and quickly sing a new song by looking at the musical score, the boy who enjoys taking things apart and putting them back together, the ten-year-old who can observe an unusual bird and draw it from memory several days later, the five-year-old who can easily dribble the ball down the court and make a basket. The truth is that *all* of these people are smart, but they express their intelligence differently.

Howard Gardner, co-director of Project Zero at Harvard University, has broadened the definition of intelligence to include seven areas:

1. **Musical intelligence**, which means such things as being able to sing on key, maintain a beat, remember music after hearing it, or compose and read songs.

2. **Interpersonal intelligence or social ability**, which means having a strong ability to enjoy friends and groups and their activities; to perceive people's moods, temperaments, motivations and intentions; and to display empathy.

3. **Spatial intelligence**, meaning having good visual memory or the ability to find one's way around, read maps, take things apart and reassemble them, or work with paints, design, light, or architectural drawings.

4. **Intrapersonal intelligence**, which involves being deeply aware of one's own feelings and thoughts, and being able to recognize and discriminate among these feelings. These people are aware of what they love and fear; they are able to insightfully talk about their own experiences and have a well-developed understanding of themselves.

5. **Bodily-kinesthetic intelligence**, or demonstrating coordination, ability and skill in both fine and gross motor movements, as with a craftsperson or athlete.

6. **Linguistic intelligence**, which means using language to communicate written and spoken meanings—to write and read. It also includes being able to word-play, rhyme, tell stories and enjoy puns.

7. **Logico-mathematical intelligence**, which includes thinking conceptually, reasoning, devising experiments, exploring abstract relationships in math, computers and logic, and noticing patterns and numbers in their environment.

Taken together, these types of intelligence provide seven ways to learn. They broaden our definition of intelligence, and in so doing, free a person to exhibit their best qualities, pursue their strengths and achieve their dreams. Parents must learn what kind of intelligences their children have in order to nurture and strengthen them and, above all, to respect their differences.

❧❧

Value and nurture every individual within your family. Discover each other's strengths, cultivate equality and respect the different types of intelligence that each brings to the group. Appreciate that each person is smart—just in diverse ways.

Tool #5: Praise Descriptively

All family members can look for the amazing attributes of each person. By paying close attention, they can help an individual see, respect and value their inner strengths. I think this is the family's most important work. But how do you help a person see her unique strengths? Reflect back. Share what you see.

Praise can be overly general and, because of this, doesn't build or strengthen self-image. Use the power of affirmations or verbal accolades—the more specific, the better. People will often simply say, "You look great" or "You did a terrific job." This praise can come across as generic; it doesn't add meaningful information. A person needs to hear how she is wonderful, in specific terms, and why.

Descriptive Praise Versus Global Praise

Specific praise is encouraging to children, teens and adults alike. Here's how this works. General praise doesn't provide enough detail to extract sufficient value from the praise. The "seed" does better with more water. There is more fruit with more specific information. It is better to point out, in detail, a number of things that might never have occurred to the person. For example, if a person explained something well to a friend, tell him that he shared some applicable facts, that he has a comfortable way of listening, that it was done in such a way that the friend could figure out some "next steps" to take, and that his personal style made the friend feel focused and positive.

General praise fails to identify and develop unique, inner strengths. The problem with this praise is that it doesn't facilitate personal learning. Describing the person's work in detail, on the other hand, adds a whole new dimension to a person's view of herself and creates a motivated learner. "Your high test score says that you studied the difficult material for a long time, understood it so well that you could apply it and were able to gain entirely new insights in the process." Here's my point: specific praise motivates and empowers. Know the power of encouragement and praise, and use it daily.

Put a WOW in your voice and praise with enthusiasm. Try out a new level of enthusiasm now. The difference in its impact will totally surprise you! Praise is not something given occasionally or on a part-time basis, but continuously, every chance you get. And don't wait to extend your praise. Give it quickly or soon after it is due.

Children—and adults too--have qualities inside them that need to be pointed out. It may take this form: "Adam, I enjoy spending time with you because you . . . (list some personal qualities) . . . you have a funny sense of humor, I feel we can talk about anything, you are very observant and have good people sense, and I can sing oldies really loudly when you're around!" Now what happens to this person if he is told—frequently—that he makes you laugh, communicates openly, has good insight into people and encourages you to sing, even when you can't carry a tune? He most likely does not get this verbal information from his peers, his siblings, or most of the adults with whom he interacts. If he hears it over and over from a significant adult, he is more likely to absorb this information. People who know their strengths and who are aware of their unique qualities become stronger and more confident. The ultimate goal is for a person to be secure in her own abilities and no longer dependent on the opinions of others. This person can say "I do these things well," and believe it!

Storing Past Accomplishments

Besides using specific detail in their praise, encourage family members and close friends to meticulously gather and store this information. They know when a person has done something particularly well. They can recall, for example, when a person managed to share her thoughts at just the right time, was able to remember critical details during an emergency situation, helped find a solution to a problem, or came up with a new idea. The encouraging family member knows these fine points or circumstances and can recall the necessary specific information from the past. This parent or family member can say, "Remember when you helped your friend find her lost term paper by walking her through her stops after school? I know you can backtrack to find your new gloves in the same way."

Think of a parent, grandparent, or other family member as the child's resource librarian, keeping the child's past accomplishments and achievements within their "shelves." They share this information with their child and provide encouragement and comfort when necessary, but especially during difficult times of growth and frustration. In this way, they help a child discover inner resources, sometimes located deep within. In this way, they can help the child do the more difficult, life-integrating work too.

> **Think of a parent, grandparent, or other family member as the child's resource librarian, keeping the child's past accomplishments and achievements within their "shelves."**

For example, when a child has been criticized by someone outside the family, the encouraging parent can help "take out the garbage" by identifying whatever aspects might be unfair or untrue, reminding the child of her strengths, then offering a plan to remedy the situation. If your child is criticized for sloppy handwriting, she needs to practice the letters on the same line. If told she has poor math skills, then maybe she needs more drills. If told she behaves rudely, then she needs to practice waiting for others to finish before speaking. If told her planning is not thorough, then she needs to put more focus and detail into future plans. If told these same plans don't include the interests of everyone involved, then she needs to build in the ideas of others. If parents can think through what specific actions need to be taken to help the child, then a strong and spirited young adult can emerge.

Use Descriptive Praise With Adults Too

There is often a dearth of the-right-kind-of-praise for adults on the home front. Descriptive praise is a technique that is not only useful with children, but works miracles on adults. It facilitates their learning and growth too! Telling an adult child that she has done a "good job" is simply not good enough. This response limits learning and growth. It would be better to point out a number of things that never would have occurred to the individual. For example, if she gave a presentation, she could be told that she helped to teach some especially important information using a very effective style of presenting material; or that it was done in such a way as to make the audience enjoy itself; or that her style left everyone feeling very unified and hopeful for improvement. This descriptive praise adds a whole new dimension to the person's view of herself and a deeper sense of motivation.

> **There is a dearth of the-right-kind-of-praise for adults on the home front. Descriptive praise is a technique that is not only useful with children, but works miracles on adults. It facilitates their learning and growth too!**

Try to give each person in your family two kinds of descriptive praise a day. Say something about their outside and their inside. Each has physical qualities and unique abilities. Notice them. Encourage this person. Give specific, detailed information as to why the person looks particularly good today or how they did a good job on something. "I really like how you're wearing your hair today." "That new breathing technique you added to your swimming stroke looks fantastic, and I'm sure it gave you the extra speed you needed to win the race." A healthy dose of descriptive praise provides one of the greatest boosts. A rewarding feeling comes from paying someone a compliment. You have become heard. Your visibility has increased. Praise, compliments and acts of kindness should not be reserved only for certain age groups. Everyone needs them.

Give Descriptive Advice on How to Improve

Parents and grandparents alike can provide older adult children who warrant constructive criticism with proactive *advice* on how to improve. Like praise, advice should be descriptive. It must specifically detail what a person can do to shore up a development need or correct a weakness. Parents and grandparents can translate constructive feedback into an action plan. For example, if a young adult has been told he is not a good writer or speaker, then the family member or close friend might recommend a specific public speaking course. If an adult child's ideas are not forward thinking, then the family member can suggest ways to weave more innovative thought into her future planning activities. If an adult child is told that her thoughts don't include the needs of a particular person or population segment, then the parent can suggest ways to work with this individual or group to build their needs into the overall picture. Rather than say, "This person has a problem—or has missed the target!" it is better to say, "This person requires some descriptive advice and a creative, well thought-out suggestion." The focus is *not* on the faults of the adult child, but on what action steps need to be completed to improve the situation. Close friends who have a well-stocked warehouse of information or knowledge of a person's past achievements can provide encouragement, comfort and constructive solutions from the "advice arena" too.

Ultimately, if a young child, teen or adult child has heard over and over again that they have special abilities and positive qualities, they are more likely to identify their own strengths and understand who they are. Everyone should be actively involved in sharing this positive information to family members.

In a nutshell: use the powerful tool of descriptive praise with all family members and friends. And don't forget to give advice on how to improve. Each person will feel loved, happy and valued when you do—and grateful! As you practice descriptive praise, your shared bond will strengthen and deepen.

Recognize the difference between descriptive praise and global praise. Give frequent and specific praise, as it motivates and facilitates learning and self-discovery. Remember: Descriptive praise and advice works miracles on adults too!

15. "R" for Renewal—Identify Specific Activities for Renewal

"The key to staying happy is really very simple. Begin by understanding your inner energies. If you look inside, you will see that when you're happy, your heart feels open and the energy rushes up inside of you. When you aren't happy, your heart feels closed and no energy comes up inside. So to stay happy, just don't close your heart."

–Michael A. Singer in *The Untethered Soul*

There are fascinating research findings on the link between sleep, vacation and relaxation and how these relate to productivity and job performance. Tony Schwartz is the CEO of "The Energy Project" and the author of *Be Excellent at Anything*. In a February 2013 *New York Times* article she noted: "Physicists understand energy as the capacity to do work. Like time, energy is finite; but unlike time, it is renewable. Taking more time off is counterintuitive for most of us. The idea is also at odds with the prevailing work ethic in most companies, where downtime is typically viewed as time wasted. More than one-third of employees, for example, eat lunch at their desks on a regular basis. More than 50 percent assume they'll work during their vacations."

> **"Like time, energy is finite; but unlike time, it is renewable."**

Schwartz goes on to note that spending more hours working often results in less sleep, which takes its toll on job performance. She notes the findings of Stanford researcher

Cheri D. Mah: When basketball players slept roughly 10 hours nightly, both their free-throw and three-point shooting increased by an average of 9 percent. Forty minute naps during the day also positively impacted air traffic controller reaction time. The accounting firm Ernst & Young completed an internal study to learn that with each additional 10 hours of vacation, year-end performance ratings improved by 8 percent. Shares Schwartz: "The importance of restoration is rooted in our physiology. Human beings aren't designed to expend energy continuously. Rather, we're meant to pulse between spending and recovering energy." Here's the cool discovery: just as we sleep in 90 minute cycles, from light to deep sleep and back out, this same cycle repeats itself during our waking ours. Similarly, suggests Schwartz, 90-minute work intervals are a prescription for maximizing our productivity. She discovered that when she writes she is most productive in the morning with three 90-miniute sessions, taking a break after each.

Find Energy From Family Love

Families can't nap, but they sure need to find renewal! But where? Can we find energy from those whom we are close to? When individuals connect in a certain way, can there be higher vibrations of energy? Though the energy generated by love may be somewhat a mystery, I believe we can learn how to nurture the powerful energy of family love. We can learn to sense this energy. It is empowering when we do because it gives us much richer information about situations and people. One way to sense energy is to generate positive energy yourself. A simple way to demonstrate this is when you smile genuinely at someone, they usually smile back, sending along positive energy in return.

The energy of family love is found in all sorts of places—vacations, on trains, in cars and sitting around the dinner table, helping others, making music, playing and physically being together, having "silly" traditions, talking and eating. One parent found this energy Christmas morning. "It's a special time when there is a spirit of anticipation and freedom. The same can be said at a celebratory dinner, perhaps when one of the family members has a birthday and everyone is around. With teenagers this 'free' family time comes late in the morning on Sunday if there is no athletic event or practice and the teens are well rested!"

One tends to always have a high amount of energy when being positive and working within the circle of love. For example, many people who I interviewed told me that when they engaged in community service, they felt it took them to a heightened place. Families are perfectly set up to experience these higher levels of energy. This is a richer, deeper place. I call it the "spirit of us."

Discover the Spirit of Us

The "spirit if us" is a dimension in which energy is distinctively different. Whether for mutual support or celebration, family members come together in one collective, cohesive unit. Rules and "shoulds" disappear. Spirits are freer. Members feel love for themselves and others. Family members become "us" rather then "you" and "me." A consciousness of "us" exists. This collective spirit is a foundation for closer relationships.

Do you ever experience times when the energy is different, where you can actually feel a special vibe when you and your loved ones are together? The family members interviewed describe this "spirit of us" energy arising from a variety of places. It was present when they focused on doing creative things together, some planned, some spontaneous, like turning the stereo up and declaring "family dance time!"

> **A consciousness of "us" exists. This collective spirit is a foundation for closer relationships.**

when they all just let loose. It was present again when they connected with each other and with nature, running around in the yard, pulling each other on the sled, having a picnic, watching a sunset on the beach, laying on their backs and watching the clouds and playing with the dog. One parent said some of the greatest happiness and laughter they experienced together came from playing games, not just board games, but ones where you must shout out an answer—the impromptu nature of these games igniting the family dynamic with kindness, acceptance, fairness, and tolerance.

Who We Are – One Family's "Energy"

For one person I interviewed, coming together for meals generated her family's energy and sense of identity: "We felt the energy was different at Church functions too, but to me, I felt it at home more. This is where we felt a kindred spirit. All of our immediate family gatherings seemed big for us, and we still make a big deal out of celebrations. My grandmother was always cooking because she had gone to culinary school and she was always catering for different events. I believe my grandmother's way to your heart was through her food. Food was at the center of our home on a daily basis. I used to tell my mother that our home was like a revolving door because there was always someone coming over due to my grandmother's food, which connected her to so many people who weren't necessarily related to us, but we would call them 'uncle,' 'aunt' or 'cousin' even if they weren't."

Her grandmother was often at the center of their family's energy. "I feel the energy of family love all of the time. My mother, father and grandmother are from the South. Although my mom came to Chicago as a very young girl, the culture and traditions that they all brought with them became instilled in our family. You sat down at breakfast, lunch and dinner together as a family. Discussions took place at the table. I remember coming home at lunch time from school and my grandmother would have lunch with me at the table before I had to go back to school. This was a time to find out how my day was going and what I was doing in school. We watched television together as a family, but television was always supervised when we were children."

Use Food, Music and Travel to Fuel Renewal

One mother talks about cultural and artistic experiences as key ingredients in producing family energy. "We were introduced to many different ethnic cuisines as children. My mother would take us out to different restaurants almost every weekend as children after our piano, ballet, tap and acting lessons. Music was also very instrumental to our family gatherings. I was told that my grandfather played the saxophone in a band before he married my grandmother. My mother and my sister played piano. I was the singer/actress. My sister and I would perform at churches, school events, concert halls, statewide and national competitions, and especially at home around family and friends growing up. Performing arts brought us together as a family. Again, it started in our home before I even began school."

They discovered this same energy through travel. She and her sister traveled almost every summer with her grandmother, even when they were very small, usually to visit relatives in Mississippi, New Orleans, California and then returning to Chicago. They loved taking the train, which at that time was called the "Super Chief" train. It took two days to get to California. The diner cars were a luxury complete with white tablecloths. She exclaimed: "These train trips were the best ever! I had my first airplane ride with my grandmother, and she used to swear that she would never ride in an airplane. I believe these family vacations and outings forged even tighter family bonds. We learned more and more about one another."

Facing Outward: Getting Away and Community Service

Another family of four finds their "sprit of us" energy when they step outside their home and household routines to enjoy a change of scenery. Let her explain: "Three of us—my husband, daughter and I—have the personality trait of working too hard and always wanting to do a good job. This self-induced stress on ourselves makes us not always 'happy campers' together. We are more worried about our individual goal to finish something rather than paying attention to each other. So the most productive way for us to feel the energy of love, all at one time, is to leave our home together – especially when there is a school break." She qualifies this time: "Even going on a car ride to Kansas City to visit my husband's very sick parents gives us time to better appreciate each other." She adds: "It's also fun on these occasions. We can get together with family cousins to play games, go hiking, ride horses, or reminisce about former times and people. The 'spirit of us': it just feels right; we don't even have to talk to each other. "

Another parent said her family feels a heightened sense of energy when they do a community service project together or help someone out. Her daughters play piano and her husband plays guitar. They experience a sense of elation when friends come over to jam—times when focus turns to the music and everyone can simply relax and have fun.

Renewal Through Play and Togetherness

The energy of family love, says another parent, comes in the spirit of play or celebration. "I think it is very special when we are together. We are sort of all over the place [geographically]. When you are physically able to be together, the energy feels different because you are playing, you are recreating, even if you are working or involved in some sort of project, you are just together." Interestingly, she feels her family experiences the joy of play more freely now that her children are grown. "When the kids were younger, I think I was so worried about just getting dinner on the table so the kids could get their homework done and get to bed on time and not be so tired and I was practically ready to drop in my tracks because of fatigue, especially if my husband was away." She adds: "They are not little children anymore and it is less about how you get from Monday to Saturday. Sometimes there is a lot of struggle, the homework, the school, the practices, and when everyone is older you are not dealing with that anymore. That is not to say that your kids are not worried about a job presentation. It is less of the nitty gritty. You have more freedom to enjoy each other."

Traditions Bring Renewal Too

Family traditions are a constant, often sacred channel for cultivating family energy. They create predictable rhythms. They bring comfort and security. They can be formal celebrations such as a Thanksgiving meal or can be small rituals like pizza and Star Trek. Traditions don't have to cost a lot of money, nor take a lot of time. They're defined simply by their ability to create closeness, constancy and continuity.

Families rally around traditions. They are an excellent source of renewal. Here are some creative ones: "We have some traditions, just silly things really. We always do waffles on Christmas Eve, that comes from me singing in church choirs for so many years and I have so many services to sing, there is no time to do a fancy dinner, just a simple one. We play charades often when we are all together. We have a blueberry pie for my birthday because we are usually on vacation in July. When the kids were little, we always did pizza on Saturday nights from a diner down the street and watched Star Trek."

One mother described when her family's energy feels heightened. "We have times together, usually having dinner and later in the dinner, when we end up sitting and talking without any effort. Everyone participates and we get into memories, and how they felt growing up, and those times were really comfortable, just happened, and there was a really good feeling." They were especially happy when her mother would come. No one was having any problems when she was there and the atmosphere was simply peaceful. She would usually come for a few days, at Thanksgiving and Easter, and sometimes in the summer, and they would have dinners together, barbeque and play games. The kids would not stay in their rooms. She was a magnet and they *always* had a good time. Joined together for celebration and fun, the "spirit of us" energy came out—and they were revitalized and renewed.

Use food, music and travel to fuel renewal. Celebrations, getting away and community service also renew, as do play, traditions, coming together and sharing memories.

Tool #6:
Record Memories—Stories, Movies, Photos and Written Correspondence

Remembering our past serves to strengthen our bond, connect us and, importantly, renew our spirit. When we observe, record and share our experiences, we invigorate the soul of the family. In a sense, we add animation. To this end, storytelling, home movies, photos and written correspondence play an epic role. They serve as imprints. They help us share the favorite moments of our past. They allow us to *peak* into our history and link us together over time. The memories and traits that are found within our network of relationships define us. Let's look closely at how storytelling, making movies, taking photos and writing to one another accomplish this substantial task. Roll em.

Tell Family Stories

When we look back at our experiences together, we can also pull out stories that have special meaning to us. This storytelling is a powerful way to express and share a family's unique history. Humor is key to my family's story selection process. Listen in on two of my favorites growing up with older brothers, and you will understand these stories' vital role.

My oldest brother Dean was a "beermeister" of sorts during his senior year of high school. He enthusiastically experimented with home brewing. His "scientific" pursuits caused some unpredicted episodes that become eventual laughter for us all. Unbeknownst to my parents, he kept the beer operation in our attic. Are you familiar with the musty smell of fermenting beer? After the first couple of days, the whole house reeked of rotten eggs. Five days later, the ale still bubbling away, there was a yeast odor at the airlock. To explain the situation Dean convinced my parents that something was wrong with the furnace. When the repairman arrived, different theories were proposed, as they all tried to figure out the cause of the stinky house. With precision, just as the repairman changed the furnace filters, Dean moved his home brewing operation to the back patio of a family friend a mile away who was gone for the winter. Perfect timing. We love to retell this story whenever we get the chance, no details withheld.

> **To this end, storytelling, home movies, photos and written correspondence play an epic role. They serve as imprints.**

The house where I grew up had a cozy fireplace in the family room. Next to it was a small compartment where wood was stored. Our winter's supply of logs could be put directly into this storage box by opening a small door at the back. Wood didn't have to be carried through the house. We simply stacked and stockpiled it in this box using the outside door. Unexpectedly, my parents slowly learned that this same double door feature also accommodated the lifestyle of teenagers. I vividly recall the year after my brother, then nineteen, had been away at college. A distinguishing feature of this age was arriving home extremely late after being out with friends. On one such night, my mother thought everyone was in the house and locked the main door. When my brother returned home, he desperately discovered that he couldn't get inside. Resourcefully, he recalled the wood box "entrance" and proceeded to come into the house through it. My mother, who was a light sleeper, heard the sounds of wood falling (as we usually kept a large supply of logs). When my brother pushed through, in the hopes of being unnoticed at three o'clock in the morning, he looked up to see her there to "greet" him. For certain, by repeating our past through storytelling, we re-experience a profound joy.

Stories like these abound in all families. Use storytelling to share much-loved moments from your own family archive. What are some of your family's favorites? Be sure to write them down. Better yet, record this special history on a video camera.

Make Home Movies

If you don't have a movie camera or a smart phone with video capabilities, buy an inexpensive, easy-to-use one. Or rent one. I did for our family's very first video recordings. For sure, movie cameras last a long time. I still have the one that I bought twenty years ago. Movies and photos become your visual memories of your family. They detail "who you are" at a point in time. But don't just use them for special occasions. Catch your everyday moments—especially moments of play and laughter.

Our oldest son, John, when he was in his early twenties, took all of our home movies and pieced different shots into various themes, like birthday parties, visits to grandparents, storytelling and play, and put them on a DVD for my husband for Father's Day. We have two such creative, thematic compilations. Each is a fascinating visual display of our family's history. I treasure them like a favorite book.

Our three now-adult sons cherish our home movies. When they return home to visit, this is one of the things they want to do—watch family movies together. We throw in popcorn and make it a fun night, as though each movie were a new release!

Their best-loved movies are the recordings of them just doing "nothing" (i.e. talking and walking and playing). What happens when we watch these videos? The entire family goes back in time. We get to see and play back the vivid detail of our growth, what we looked like long ago, how we talked and walked and played, and how we all interacted together. Last year, I made each son a digital copy of all of our home videos, putting them altogether on a large-memory flash drive as a holiday gift. They now each have a complete copy of our theatrical history! Extraordinarily important, these peaks into the past give us access to those moments in time in which families make contact with the soul.

> **Our three now-adult sons cherish our home movies. When they return home to visit, this is one of the things they want to do—watch family movies together. We throw in popcorn and make it a fun night, as though each movie were a new release!**

Take Photos

Besides family movies, photos naturally serve as reminders of our fun together. The qualities they illustrate (some quirky and some common) launch us into memories that we hold dear, and always generate hoots of laughter. They are the jewels or precious metals of all families. Don't miss out on them. They too will become your entertainment of choice for years to come.

Two of my favorite photos of my mother were of she in costume: dressed up as a green sea monster in one, dressed as a water heater in another—both taken with my Aunt Ann, who too sported this same goofy party wardrobe. Their sea monster hair was rope they had dyed green along with some long johns that completed the outfit. The goo they smeared on their hands and face was made from egg whites and green food coloring. I for one would have skipped this part! I guess they felt they needed to look authentic.

Green sea monsters

As for the water heaters, they were the real deal. They got some old discarded ones from our neighbor who was a plumber. The white puffs at the square opening (where their heads popped out) were lacey toilet seat covers, which they used to cover their faces. The real pipes sticking out in the back made it difficult for them to walk and obviously to sit down, so my dad transported the two of them to the luncheon party in the bed of his truck. Both adventures were a pretty big deal for all of us kids and are probably why I still remember some of these details. I look at these photos often, and go back to that time when I was six years old and think to myself, "now I understand where I got my strangely odd sense of humor!"

I have another tattered photo, vintage 1928, of my mom with her high school basketball team. Lined up with seven girls and one coach, she was the tallest and thinnest, and was called "Soup Bone." Friends and family often reminded her of this nickname. Even at 100 years old, her height and slimness were enduring trademarks, as was her still zippy little walk, all recaptured in an old photo.

I keep a stack of these photos on my desk. When I shuffle through them I see a shot of two of our then-young sons, with their trademark water guns in hand and red boots on foot; another of my husband and I at a picnic on the day before our wedding, taken at the bridge below a high waterfall where he proposed to me; one of the priest who married us smiling at this same picnic; another of us dancing at our wedding in my parents' back yard; still another of my dad waving as he mowed the lawn to get ready for the wedding; one of my parents huddled closely with our two oldest sons when they were small; another of our young sons swimming while on vacation; another of my dad on his 80th birthday in his bathrobe with two of our sons sitting on each side; and one of my mom, then almost 100 years old, hugging our youngest son when he was twenty. These photos let me peak into the past, see different ages and look back to different times. The entire batch of photos helps me tap into memories and traits and connect with our network of family relationships. Looking at them results in a phenomenal experience. My simple takeaway: Keep photos around you and regularly look through the stack. You will jump for joy.

> **Keep photos around you and regularly look through the stack. You will jump for joy.**

Spending time with grandparents is another quick and easy way to experience and learn family history. Grandma and grandpa have all the stories and memories stored right there for us to enjoy. Hang out with them to catch the colorful details of your family culture, traditions and relationships. Better yet, use your video camera to record their stories and their image for years to come.

Written Correspondence

Six months after my mom died, my two brothers and sister-in-law and I got together at her home for three days of serious sorting. Mind you, my parents lived in this house for over sixty-five years. Keep in mind, I was with one brother who had been a beer brewmeister growing up, and another brother who liked to consume this same beverage, and you will understand the backdrop. This is to say, we were serious with our tasks at hand, but we also wanted it to be a lot of fun. While many things occurred during this three-day time span, it was the written correspondence that served as a floodgate for reflection, renewal and, yes, personal "analysis." Let me explain. Early on we each unearthed a plethora of letters from our high school and college days, correspondence from both of our parents and from past boyfriends and girlfriends. One brother went to bed one night with a stack of these letters on his pillow. When he awoke sleepy-eyed early the next morning, he announced: "I have finally figured out my life. It all seems to make sense to me now." Reading his old letters had helped him make connections, understand relationships and do some self-reflection, which life at close-up and full-speed did not afford.

As our sorting efforts continued and we realized everything had been preserved for us to review, from birth through our early twenties, we were exceedingly grateful for this piecing-together-life opportunity. We had many "ah hah" moments, renewing and reflecting on the past with curiosity and newfound understanding. For example, we each uncovered our complete collection of college posters, which had adorned our walls during these formative years. Think Janis Joplin, the musical *Hair*, and quotes by e. e. cummings. These wall posters served as correspondence too, affording us additional memories, laughter and recognition.

We also discovered audio correspondence. There were six tapes, the old reel type, which were sent back and forth when I was twenty-years-old and lived in Vienna, Austria for a year. Disturbingly, during our hectic organizing, they were put in the sizeable outside iron dumpster, the kind you see when a home is remodeled. Realizing this mistake, my brother Paul kindly volunteered to help me sort through the already-tossed items, using a five-foot ladder to climb into the huge bin. If you saw our dirty faces and clothes after a half-dozen frantic attempts to find the magical audio tapes, you will understand the importance of preserving these memories, which I am happy to share we recovered.

Since travel was discussed earlier as a source of renewal, let me share another eye opener during our big sort. We discovered a prominent drawer in my parent's living room where they kept *everything* from their past almost-seventy years of travel. Opening this chest was like accompanying them on a trip. They had saved all kinds of travel correspondence--brochures, itineraries, destination events, menus, travel guides, concerts stubs and museum passes. The detail was spectacular. It gave us the unusual opportunity to revisit their play over the years together—from honeymoon to sunset—reminding me of the powerful role that play has in refueling and renewing the spirit.

Make family imprints and create memories together. Tell stories, make movies, take photos and save correspondence to share favorite moments from your past. These memories bring happiness and connection, strengthen the family bond and liven up—often with comic amusement—the shared history. In remembering our past we invigorate the soul of the family for the future.

Tool #7:
Identify Family Values and Rituals

Values and rituals are the essence of a family's culture. Attend to each in a deliberate way and the bond will deepen. Here are some ways to first uncover, share and live-by agreed upon values and, second, to create enduring family rituals.

Live By Agreed-Upon Values

Shared values are essential. Observes a mother of an autistic son: "We could not have survived without our faith. Our Catholic faith is essential to the soul of our family. So many times all we had was prayer and surrender. At those brinks, we were emptied. That emptying left us focused on the values that are essential to us: honesty, kindness, patience (in spades), feeling and expressing love, and acceptance." She added: "We keep true to the thoughts and behaviors that represent our values, and we are accountable to each other. The last value is humor. We make each other laugh by finding whatever is screwy, even in the depths." Powerful and profound, our values guide and unite us.

If families talk about their values, it helps them prioritize what is important to each member *and* it helps to identify what emotions and feelings and interests we share. Talking about values helps each person touch others in a heart-to-heart way and understand what is at the core of their priorities and beliefs. Often we know we have values, but we can't put them into words.

> **Often we know we have values, but we can't put them into words.**

Pick a fun spot, like in front of a fireplace or outside on a warm summer night. Ask every family member, including young children, what is most important to them. Have them write it down, or if they are too young, write it down for them. Then share these values. The first time we did this as a family, I learned that basketball and summer vacations were important to my nine-year-old and spending time with friends was important to my older teen. Their "values" helped me understand how to best use our time, look after their needs and make decisions about what we should do together.

The way to reach consensus is by first finding full agreement on the values. This process requires defining and discussing the strengths, weaknesses, advantages and disadvantages of conflicting values. The group must make a decision on the ultimate values to be accepted. The parent cannot step in and close the discussion or make a unilateral decision. This would defeat the ownership building process. Consensus building should be viewed as the glue to bond individual values together within a family.

As we know, individuals bring their own personal values with them into the family scene. Undoubtedly, individuals will express conflicting values. This is exactly why the process needs to give people time to think about differing values, reconcile them with their own, shift some of their thinking and strive to find common ground. Consensus building should enable individual values to be strengthened, endorsed and embraced by the family. Family consensus is an essential process that requires listening and selecting values that best define what is important for the group.

As families, we can discover each other's values. I think that both parents and kids like to get involved in discovering values. Here is, first, a description of a user-friendly "Values Discovery" chat to find out about each other's values, and second, a how-to approach for consensus building within a family. When each member feels that his or her individual beliefs and ideas have been incorporated into the group, then greater consensus is built.

Values Discovery and Consensus

Let me share with you what happened when one family with teenage sons and a ten-year-old sat by the fire one cold, snowy night. They had lots of fun writing down their individual values and then talking about them. Both teenagers identified freedom as a key value, as you will see from their lists below. The sixteen-year-old said he valued honesty, kindness, happiness and joy, close relationships with great friends and family, belief in oneself, perseverance, balance and yin/yang, knowledge and experience, purity, individuality, good health and freedom; he liked nature, the ocean, computers and the rush and excitement of surfing, karate and running. The fourteen-year-old identified dancing, friends, family, beaches, hot breakfast, laughing, reading a good book, listening to music and freedom, which he described as the ability and prerogative to make his own decisions. The ten-year-old valued basketball, the ocean, legos, friends, winter and J.R.R. Tolkien "stuff." Their father valued respect and consideration for others, belief in diversity, the power of love, trust, family, individuality and self-esteem. Their mother valued time for relaxation and no stress, deep friendships, nature, family fun and togetherness, intimate conversations, self-growth and spiritual understanding.

After each family member identified and listed their individual values, each took a very close look at them. Then, each person selected the five top values from their list and wrote them down. Each family member proceeded to talk about his or her values with everyone listening. Next, they decided as a group which individual values should be adopted as the "family values." This didn't mean that those individual values not selected by the group should be abandoned. They would remain important to that individual, but the family would now have its own unique set of values, based on the input of all its members.

When this family developed a set of family values in this way, they came up with a "Family's Shared Values" list. It is comprised of ten special values, unique to this family, posted in a visible spot for all to frequently see. Their values list includes:

- Recognize the importance of relationships with family and close friends.
- Make special time for nature, especially the ocean, for its beaches and surfing.
- Find time to read, listen to music and walk regularly.
- Pursue our individual special interests, including swing dancing, legos, computers, karate, running and basketball.
- Have the freedom to make one's own decisions, believe in oneself and persevere.
- Find daily balance and spiritual understanding.
- Build self-esteem in each other.

- See individuality as a strength. Each person is unique and should be respected.

- See the power of love, trust, kindness, honesty and knowledge.

- Seek laughter, happiness, joy and hot breakfast!

This method can help families discover their shared values. Not only will there be clarity and fun when they do, but the bond will deepen.

Create Family Rituals

What are your fondest memories from childhood? For many, they are the things that your family did together on a regular basis. These rituals serve as touchstones in your life. Not only are they comforting, but they too become lasting memories for your family and for subsequent generations. Often they develop around birthdays or family get-togethers. Or they take place around meals, favorites restaurants, family songs, TV shows, movies and holidays—the list is endless.

Think back to the pattern of your early morning routine when you were small. My dad got up at 6:00 a.m., read the newspaper and then cooked the entire family bacon and eggs. When breakfast was ready, he woke us all up and we sat there in our jammies and enjoyed his delightful meal. At about 8:15 a.m. he drove us to school in an old yellow Studebaker that had a hole drilled in the bottom of the floor, an "invention" of sorts to let the rainwater out! This was Oregon, mind you. Whenever we turned the corner the water moved from one side to the other and out the hole. Often it didn't work too well and we had to lift our feet not to get our shoes wet.

I am sure you have your own family morning rituals. Every family creates them. Rituals are the ways that we do things in the everyday life of the family. They include the way we eat, when we eat, whether we sit together at dinner or in front of the TV. They also include the way we play, talk, laugh and touch. All rituals are learned. Change your morning rituals and see what happens! It soothes the mind and heart to know that some activities can always be counted on.

Understand the Role of Family Culture

Family culture, to me, is a state of mind. It's the way that family members behave and communicate with each other. This mental information gets translated into a specific set of actions, communications and responses. Each ritual is learned by and shared with family members over time. Cultural rituals are unique to each family. Each group has their own signals too. These are a series of verbal, physical and emotional signs, exclusive to the family. Parents and children mentally decipher the signals that they receive daily from each other and emotionally translate their meaning. Family culture is coded into are brains as well as our hearts.

This is why it is also so difficult to change culture. The norms and values that exist in the family become the group's cultural rules and beliefs. Specific norms and values are exchanged from one member to another by group interaction. Culture is passed on in this way.

Parents can get stuck in the old way of doing things on the family front. Perhaps they've done what their own parents did. They have imitated or mirrored their family's values, attitudes, rituals and themes, rather than rethink, adapt and tailor them to fit their own unique family. We live in a constantly changing world and contemporary life has provided us with a huge array of choices. Rather than automatically adopting the prevailing cultural rituals, values and norms, everyone can participate in developing their own. The sparkling insights and perspectives of children can be a powerful stimulus.

Identify Three Family Rituals

Any event the family enjoys and does regularly can be a ritual. It might be a fancy Friday dinner or a regular walk up the local mountain. The best part is that there are no rules on how to define rituals. They just have to make you and your family feel special.

Form your rituals thoughtfully. Consider the following: Most families are so busy during the week that they never sit down to eat together. A typical weeknight might have two or three family members gather for dinner, followed by two more when they arrive home at a later hour. Staged eating isn't bad, as it may be necessary given the juggle of school and jobs. But a uniting ritual could be around a meal—perhaps to eat together just *one* time during the week, even if it is breakfast or on a weekend. Some families cook together as their ritual, once a month or for a holiday. Another ritual could be to throw an annual party for friends, adults and kids alike. Another could be to do something creative as a family every year, like paint of picture together, which is one of our favorites. This involves the entire family painting together on a single canvas with each member selecting a portion of it. Be sure to date it and hang it for all to see.

Be imaginative when inventing your family's rituals. They have the power to strengthen and deepen your relationships, to carve out a fun, distinctive culture and to interweave each person's unique attitudes, interests and feelings. The challenge is to accommodate each family member and find something that resonates with everyone. One person, for example, likes vacations that involve adventurous travel, while another prefers to read and relax. Form your family's rituals with considerable care. Rituals act like glue that holds the family together. Parents and children

Do something creative as a family every year, like paint of picture together, which is one of our favorites. This involves the entire family painting together on a single canvas with each member selecting a portion of it. Be sure to date it, and hang it for all to see.

One person, for example, likes vacations that involve adventurous travel, while another prefers to read and relax. Form your family's rituals with considerable care. Rituals act like glue that holds the family together. Parents and children become the creators of a distinctive family culture with unique rituals. Arrange yours thoughtfully.

become the creators of a distinctive family culture when rituals are arranged thoughtfully.

Talk about your family's values, prioritize what is important to each member and seek consensus to generate a shared family value set. Understand the role that culture plays in a family and use this to create enduring family rituals.

16. "T" for Togetherness— Make Togetherness Tangible

"Go to a restaurant, sip a glass of wine, listen to some jazz, or take a hike. Go outdoors and come back and have a pizza, nothing fancy, just time really. It is the gift of time, not so much the activity. That is really what it is all about. You can buy things, but you can't buy time. Time is finite."

–An older parent

"In the attitude of silence the soul finds the path in a clearer light, and what is elusive and deceptive resolves itself into crystal clearness. Our life is a long and arduous quest after truth."

–Ghandi

"There is a community of the spirit. Join it and feel the delight of walking in the noisy streets and being the noise. Close both eyes to see with the other eye."

–Rumi

One of the great mysteries of family is that while we are all different, we can find places of commonality and unity. Family is a place where members are committed *both* to the individual and to the whole, where each voice is heard and valued and the group may come together for love, acceptance and togetherness.

Create Quiet Times of Togetherness

The feeling of togetherness can be powerful—and it can be quiet or noisy! Let's look first at quietly shared times. In one of my favorite books, *The Enchantment of Everyday Life,* author Thomas Moore says that "silence is not an absence of sound but rather a shifting of attention towards sounds that speak to the soul…the most important sounds in a person's life may be so quiet that they are easily missed." Just as we care for our individual soul by taking a walk in the woods or along the ocean, we can care for the soul of the family within the ordinary and everyday too by finding quiet moments during the day. Let me share two favorites from my childhood that I continually re-experience in my mind as I have become older. The first is the memory of sitting outside with my dad on the patio late at night. The night air was fresh and cool. We didn't talk. We simply sat in the darkness, just the two of us, soaking up the quiet. At times we heard the stream at the end of the yard. There was no expectation to visit. We both sat together and enjoyed one another's company. The quiet brought us closer together in the stillness of the night air.

Second, any chance I could I'd jump into my dad's pickup truck and drive with him to visit some farmland that he loved about twenty minutes from our home. We didn't talk much on our car ride other than his occasionally pointing out various kinds of crops and telling me interesting facts about them. And once we got there we didn't do much, except walk around, trying not to get stuck, truck or shoes, in the thick clay mud. His love of this land and the quiet pervading this experience created a sense of intimacy.

When my own children were young, they too loved taking this trip with their grandfather, or "papa" as he was so affectionately called. My son James is fond of sharing the story of when he and my dad got stuck in the mud in the same pickup truck. They ended up hiking some distance together in search of someone to help dig them out. Along the way, my dad discov-

I am curious to discover what my own children will select as the soulful quiet moments of their childhood as they get older.

ered that he left his wallet at home. So he made a trade, offering a six-pack of coke for a lift out of the slippery muck.

I think we must seek out soulful experiences, become comfortable with silence, and honor our quiet times together. I am curious to discover what my own children will select as the soulful quiet moments of their childhood as they get older.

How does your family carve out quiet time together? A few parents shared their efforts. Sometimes this involved just being in the moment with each other, enjoying silence together. Quiet moments often occur in connection with nature, like watching a sunset, hanging out in the yard, laying on the ground, or looking at the clouds. Books played a huge role in family togetherness, especially when children were young and read together. One person shared her family's success: "It is easy to carve out quiet time. We can still be in the same room. It is not unusual for us to be together and one person is reading, two other people are talking to one another, and someone else is looking at the television. Then, all of a sudden someone says

THE SOUND OF SILENCE

> **"It is easy to carve out quiet time. We can still be in the same room. It is not unusual for us to be together and one person is reading, two other people are talking to one another, and someone else is looking at the television. Then, all of a sudden someone says something and we are talking about that subject. We are good at multitasking."**

something and we are talking about that subject. We are good at multitasking."

Another family described their togetherness as a portfolio of shared activities. "We enjoy things like cooking together, eating out, going to movies, walking, hiking and going to museums. We often read and share snippets with each other. Those are our quieter times, in between all the hustle and bustle of regular life." Quiet can be a pause against confusion, not necessarily an absence of sound.

Make Noise Together—Celebrate Holidays, Birthdays and Special Meals

Like quiet, noise can also be soothing to the soul. Our neighbor's old dog, Forrest (as in Gump), affectionately howls periodically thoroughout the day. When I am writing for long periods of time I often try to figure out if there is a pattern to his surprisingly serene sounds, some resembling a calming trumpet and others a dangling drum. What might appear as noise to others may bring calm and peace, even relaxation, to those who routinely experience this noise. Adult children, for example, can effortlessly pull up "noisy" memories form their childhood—the popping sound of the morning coffee pot or people moving around downstairs after they've gone up for the night. When I was a teenager, I loved the loud bolstering laughter that resonated from my parent's dinner parties. Like city buses that increase in frequency during rush hour, these parties increased in frequency as we went away to college! Since I was the youngest and last to leave, I witnessed these lively gatherings and sounds of friends who had simply come for fun and play. Their noise and energy were contagious. Like dinner parties, weddings often turn up the noise in a positive way too. I have often felt that there is a parallel relationship—the noisier the wedding, the superior the celebration. Witness the dancing and whooping at the next wedding you attend and weigh in on the value of noise to the celebrative soul.

Our family gatherings involved lots of relatives, easily fifty and often more. Picture a healthy number of cousins, aunts and uncles, with an equal number of children to adults. (There were six siblings in my mom's family and five in my dad's). Family holidays were like a ruckus party—fun, thunderous and lively. My childhood memory of them is running non-stop, having fun and being wild without typical adult supervision. Although certainly present, the adults were not on my radar. They were having their own fun.

In my family birthday parties meant presents, cake and the celebration of the person, and included an elaborately planned, well-prepared, scrumptious, large meal. Also, other special days, like Valentines Day, Mother's Day and Father's Day each had their unique to-dos and distinctive festivity and merrymaking programs and rituals. The connective tissue among all those events was the simple fact of our living together.

Just as holidays and birthdays were grand affairs, each day was celebrated with three nutritious meals served with everyone sitting together as a family. Meals took on extraordinary importance. This is because my mom loved to cook. She was a home economics major at Oregon State University in the early 1930s. Meals, too, had significance in the car, which was always our mode of vacation travel. Regularly, we ate a three-course meal on a ten-hour non-stop car trip. Both of my parents adamantly believed this was the only way to travel. Eating in the car was essential to the trip's success, did not need to be terribly fancy and was always fun and appealing. Think avocados sliced on crackers, tiny hot dogs from that little can and cookies for dessert, and you are good to go.

Use Food As A Unifier

Another family carved out family time around food. "Our family gatherings mainly consist of my mom, sister, niece and me. Food is still the essential ingredient to our gatherings. We cook together. Sometimes we just get together to talk and catch up, or watch a movie." She adds: "We love to share what is happening in our lives and, because my mother is retired, she loves to listen to our stories. We are always meeting at my house because my mom and I live together. We sometimes go out to restaurants together. We entertain one another. We celebrate each other's successes. We don't perform for one another in our living room like we used to when we were kids, but laughter is still at the center of our gatherings."

Food in fact played a huge role in our family togetherness. To this day I catch myself passing recipes forward, asking for recipes and making recipes from friends and family alike. There is never a lot of precision here. Grammy's famous chocolate pie calls for a "heaping spoonful of chocolate." My mom's apple crisp asks for two generous tablespoons of flour. Continual note to self: relax and have fun while cooking and never get hung up on the details. I had a little electric play stove when I was six years old. A future foodie and soon-to-be entrepreneur, I recycled the flat piece of bubble gum that came inside a pack of baseball cards, innovatively placed it on a tiny cookie sheet, put it in my toy oven, heated it up and served it piping hot for five cents throughout the neighborhood. Note to the business world: this was called a huge profit, as the baseball cards themselves cost five cents. I also sold chocolate (often not terribly fresh) that I had saved from gifts and past birthdays and holidays in my little store, also for a handsome price increase as well. To sum up, this young business was fun and inclusive, just like our family's more traditional get-togethers.

In my own family we have tried to nurture cooking skills. I figured out that children don't learn how to cook by watching—they have to do it! My husband and I readily shared the kitchen with all three boys. One of the best results is that now we can sit back and let them cook for us! We have our favorite meals, one of the most memorable being our clam chowder that we all make together on Christmas Eve. An observer of our kitchen scene might be surprised at our industrious and methodical activity. The five of us participate equally in preparing and cooking our chowder. We all know what's in it. Any one of us could make it without the cherished recipe. Yet, to be sure, with five "chefs" assiduously involved, our chowder never tastes quite the same from year to year. Once the flour and butter roux wasn't added to the hot milk at the right time and it curdled. Another year we tossed out the clam juice instead of adding it to the pot! Another year we undercooked the potatoes. The last two years we have added fresh clams. We've learned that if we add all the different ingredients, the flavors blend together and it tastes incredibly sensational, very rich and healthy too. Like our annual clam chowder, experiment together in your kitchen. It will always make for hearty family relationships, especially if you have lots of chefs.

Discover Your Own Togetherness Formulas—Find Little Opportunities to Connect

Here's another family's activity mix: "Dinnertime is a small celebration each day when we can share what has happened, encourage each other and consider how to solve problems. For quiet time at home, we have family movie night. Travelling offers quiet times for us. We go to my brother's home where his family lives in the woods where everyone is happy doing nothing together or making some new adventure like getting kissed by wolves or looking for bears or horseback riding and hiking." She continues: "Birthdays are dinners at home together. Big birthdays are bigger parties at home. We like family parties where we invite other entire families. We enjoy grilling and picnicking outside. When we travel, we like to save some special time for the beach between our must-see museums and sites. Celebrating includes the theatre too and occasionally eating out together."

Said another family spokesperson: "Birthdays are always big celebrations for us. We always have our own family birthday celebration and then will do a bigger dinner with extended family. Because both girls have summer birthdays, five days apart, we always have a daylong celebration." She adds: "A couple summers ago we went to Universal Studios to Harry Potter Land because both girls are major Harry Potter fans. We love Christmas; my husband picks out the Christmas tree, my daughters and I decorate the tree and house and we always have friends over to make tons of gingerbread house cookies. This year, two little girls moved into the house next door and their mom is from Turkey and had never decorated cookies so we had them all over. The girls and I always look forward to those traditions. And we always deliver gifts and food Christmas morning then leave for a three-hour drive to my sister's house." As for their quiet time, "the only way to get my husband not to work is to physically go somewhere. So we go on family vacations a couple times a year to just all be together without television or phones, usually a beach somewhere."

Tap Into Your Creativity to Find Bonding Ideas

Over time these shared activities—both small and large—coalesce into our family bonds. But it is best not to take oneself too seriously, as these anecdotes convey. About thirty years ago one large extended family got together for their grandmother's 70th birthday. The group included four children, their spouses and fifteen grandchildren. One of the adults, a creative playful guy, would invent new games when the family got together. His games typically involved geography. But on this trip he happened to notice a dead pelican with the grandkids washed up on the beach and he invented the "Dead Pelican Society," complete with secret meetings and a special handshake. Pelicans represent fidelity, industriousness and generosity, and are symbolic in early Christianity in that they feed their young with their own blood! Now, twenty years later, the "Dead Pelican Society" selects new young members among the grandchildren. This creative and playful bonding activity was shared among the younger "rising stars" of the family, and served to nurture inclusion among the younger ranks.

Another family comes together around a regular book club, expanding friendships while reading books together. Ages range from thirty-five to almost seventy. The group includes the three adult children (two of whom were co-founders), their parents and friends brought in along the way. There are now thirteen in the group. They try to meet once a month. After reading sixty-five books together, they had a party. One of the co-founders located all the books online and made a slide show of each book cover. She had bookmarks, quotes from reading and memory books for everyone to take home. When they meet, usually on a Sunday, they have lunch at a book-related location. When they read *Secretariat,* they went to the Arlington racetrack for lunch. When they read *A Gift from the Sea*, they put out a little wading pool in their backyard and had dad be the chef!

And finally, two parents shared their set of bonding activities that bring their family together. First, "We celebrate with brownies, ice cream, cake and just about anything fattening! S'mores over a campfire, homemade chocolate cookies… anything that can get the kids to the table after school. Or a meatloaf for dinner creates a celebration." A father shared: "When I exchange texts with my sons or they are exchanging texts with each other, we end each message with the letters 'hs' which means 'handshake!' We created this ourselves as a term of endearment between boys and men! As a family my wife and I encourage laughter; we buy small gifts for each other; we have dinner around the table; we walk and cycle together; we listen to inspiring music together; we listen to our sons play their instruments; we have always read bedtime stories to our sons, and our youngest son, who is ten, now reads us poems and other stories; we have interesting conversations together and if we see someone within the family who is struggling, we make time for them immediately."

Create quiet times of togetherness—and noisy ones too. Make a big deal about grand celebrations—holidays, birthdays and other special days. Use food as a unifier. Discover your own togetherness formulas and tap into your creativity to find bonding ideas.

Tool #8:
Listen Selflessly, Talk Deeply

Listen Selflessly

What is deep listening? It's when you listen carefully without judging. It can feel like touching. Weaving relationships together is all about listening. Explore and develop your own abilities to listen better. The deeper you listen, the better you feel and the more you experience the fibers that make up the relationship cloth.

We listened deeply when we were children. This is how we learned as infants, then as toddlers and young children. Unfortunately, when we became adults, many of us stopped hearing. We focused instead on talking about our own ideas and ourselves—neither listening nor asking questions. Adults need to jump-start their deep listening abilities and recover this lost skill.

How do we renew and improve our deep listening? Practice, practice, practice. The family offers many opportunities for active listening. It is a prerequisite for sharing ideas, feelings and values. Listening skills are critical to developing meaningful relationships, especially friendships, within the family.

Deep listening is rare. Within the family, members can learn to listen compassionately. An active listener will communicate that they are with you in any number of ways. Most speakers know whether active listening has occurred. Oddly, adults will often continue talking even when there are no signs that someone is listening! They have forgot how to observe the listener. Parents can learn from children how to listen more deeply.

What are some "indicators" or signs that someone is actively listening to what you are saying? The listener expresses feelings of warmth and enthusiasm or extends physical contact or a smile. Acknowledgment is a key action that can signal compassionate listening. The listener's eyes are alert and they nod their head. They ask questions or verbally acknowledge that they have understood an idea. They may add information, get closer to you physically, or ask others to join the group. Good listeners also apply the general information they hear to related situations.

Check your own listening skills. Ask yourself: Am I attentive? Do I accept the speaker and the situation? Do I clarify and try to understand? Are my views changing or being supported? If you follow these guidelines, you will learn to listen more deeply.

The Power of Two-way Communication

Communication is essential to the family bond. One parent reflected: "I feel the presence of the bond, healthy or weak, all the time. This feeling is continually with me. If we are communicating, sharing, supporting, or interacting, it is strong. Other times, it doesn't seem to be working very well. When people stop sharing what is going on in their lives, when assumptions are made that aren't true, it is not such a great place."

Communication is not easy. We put up walls to protect ourselves, we prefer privacy in regard to certain subjects and we fear judgment. The give-and-take process of communication is difficult not only for children but adults too. Unavoidably, communication is sometimes poor, members get stuck, or someone feels left out.

Everyone has to work together to keep a family bond healthy. Reflected one astute grandmother, "You have to keep communicating and you have to have compassion. If you are going to be down on somebody because you are not happy with that person, and if you don't talk about it, then you get stuck. If the communication is strong, then the bond becomes stronger. When somebody gets left out in family gatherings, or doesn't participate for whatever reason, the bond is impacted." To prevent this from happening, family members must learn to talk deeply and listen selflessly. Each practice serves to strengthen relationships and deepen the bond.

Talking is critical to learning because it increases understanding. John Dewey, the well-known educational philosopher, said that learning involves the re-presentation of one's experiences. When we encourage a child or teen to talk in a group setting—family or school—the child learns. The child or teen re-presents her experiences and begins to understand them. And when a child hears other children and adults talking, her pool of possibilities enlarges. The same is true with adults! They need to process too, and talking deeply helps us all learn.

Learning how to talk to one another may be the single most important thing we can do to create a strong family. Imagine what family settings would be like if there was no talking. This happens in strict families where children are afraid to say anything, so there is silence. Communication gaps exist in most families, and communication that is honest and respectful can be rare. Yelling, one of the worst forms of communication, is too common. Healthy families are built through frequent, careful, two-way communication—lots of talking—with one another.

The Energy of Openness

Talk can be a powerful tool. Haim Ginott, author of *Teacher and Child*, said: "How parents and teachers talk tells a child how they feel about him. Their statements affect his self-esteem and self-worth. To a large extent, their language determines his destiny." It's important that talk be boundless, unrestricted and deep. Parents often feel safer when conversation falls within familiar territory, but children, especially teens, need deep conversations, as do young adults. Don't miss out on this powerful way to get closer. It can be very nourishing. Initiate new topics. Dream out loud. Explore different subjects. Children and teens have a lot of fears, as do adults. Talking openly can help immensely.

Learning how to talk deeply creates a rare and wonderful *energy*. As parents, we must help open and create channels for talking. Describe problems, give information, encourage dialogue and don't forget to model how to do it. Fully express your own feelings, needs and expectations. Even share flaws. Talk about everything and nothing. Share past experiences and what was learned from them. It will inspire children to share theirs, now and as they get older.

> **It's important for parents to walk down unfamiliar conversational paths.**

It's important for parents to walk down unfamiliar conversational paths. Opening up different topics, even ones you're not certain of, can lead to rich conversational experiences. It will create rare friendships with children, teens and adults. Happy as well as sad experiences can be shared. Break free from old and repeated topics. It's good to change your conversational patterns. Exchange thoughts and private tears and explore perspectives on everything—from friends to fears. Discuss an issue as if it were your last chance to do so.

Encourage your child to talk and talk, and challenge yourself to listen carefully. Try to do this on a regular basis, perhaps at dinner. You may establish a ritual where all family members, children, parents and even invited friends, go around the table and talk about the most meaningful—or discouraging—part of their day. This may be an event at school or work, a personal project, or a thought —anything that has special importance. Happy as well as sad experiences can be shared during this time.

Talking through touch is also a powerful form of communication. It immediately lets a child, teen, or adult know that you love her. It allows you to feel the unique bond and energy between you. It eliminates distance. A daily ritual can be established which includes: looking in their eyes, squeezing their hand, saying: "Have I told you today how much I love you." This same communication is valuable between each parent too and can have a powerful impact on your relationship.

❧❧

Renew, improve and practice your deep listening skills. Selfless, compassionate listening is a prerequisite for sharing ideas, feelings and values—and is critical to developing meaningful relationships. Talking deeply creates a rare and powerful energy. Close and healthy families are built through frequent, honest, two-way talk with one another—and lots of it!

17. "S" for Struggle—Find the Silver Linings

"Someone I loved once gave me a box full of darkness. It took me years to understand that this, too, was a gift."

—American poet Mary Oliver

If struggle knocks at the family door, and it surely will, soulful experiences may also be at hand. If we embrace the struggle and acknowledge the hard work ahead, family relationships have the power to grow, change and even transform. Through struggle the family can become more closely connected and the shared bond can deepen. Struggle is a stimulus for connection. In the words of Mary Oliver above, it can be a gift.

Struggle Strengthens or Weakens the Family Soul

For one family, the soul manifests itself through their autistic son. "His presence in our lives, and the way we each have responded to the challenge of his disability, is what makes us unique as a group." The family came together to work with autism. The soul can be discovered through conflict or struggle, as with this family, which so often experiences the brink of emotion and sanity. "We had to dig deeply into our resources to respond and survive."

Conflict, struggle and pain can strengthen or tear apart the soul of a family. Through courage, tenacity, patience and the resourcefulness of each member, the burden and struggle can be alleviated with honesty, creativity and wit. Whether a family member is chronically ill, terminally ill, mentally ill, or an addict, the family as a whole is put to life's test. Many families cannot tolerate the stress of such issues. Denial of a problem can isolate family members. Anger, betrayal, frustration, fear and terror are powerful emotions that can fracture a family bond and wound the family soul. Disagreements over a problem can lead to stress, conflict and struggle. Without patience, love, endurance and strength, the family soul can become deeply damaged and the family spirit can be

smothered. But resources both in and outside the family can help to outlast stress and overcome conflict. The family soul can survive and actually begin to thrive as family members find the resolve to take on life's difficult situations.

Struggle Exists Everywhere

Struggle, then, is a part of all families. I don't know of any family where struggle is not a part of the family dynamics. If for some reason a family has not had some type of struggle, inevitably it will land on the doorstep. Struggle is ubiquitous. It may not be readily shared, but once conflict surfaces, you may become a witness, ally and guide to a friend or family member's struggles. Here are a few examples of common family challenges that arose in my research: painful exclusion of a family member from the group, the paradoxical journey of drug and alcohol addiction, money struggles, and disagreements over priorities and ways of addressing problems. Secrecy, disappointments, chronic depression and divorce are only a few additional struggles. The list can go on and on. As one mother shared: "I have struggled early on as a young mother. Sometimes one parent is not at home. So I had lots of time thinking about single parenting and struggling, head barely above water. It was painful just doing it on my own."

Enduring Change and Loss

I have yet to mention the particularly acute life struggles, such as a child loosing a parent or a parent loosing a child or an aging mother loosing her mental faculties. Loss and pain are everywhere and a part of the human condition. One parent summed up her family's struggles, large and small: "Together, we have experienced the death of three parents/grandparents. We have suffered from unexpected job loss, breakdown of a relationship and the failure to be chosen for an important dance role or theater part. Conflict and pain have brought us closer together as a shared common experience in our own group. It's part of what has defined us as a family."

Another family member reflects: "I'm sure, like most families, it is difficult to single out one particular struggle or conflict that our family has gone through. We, like many families, have endured many deaths, illnesses, divorces and financial struggles. I guess the biggest ongoing event is watching as my very beautiful, proud and independent mother grows older. She is slowly not being able to remember or recall like she used to. Even though she can still drive and do a lot for herself, she suffers from mild cognitive impairment." She observes: "This has changed the dynamics of the family because it is no longer mom who is doing everything for everybody else. It is now our turn to take care of

> **"Together, we have experienced the death of three parents/ grandparents. We have suffered from unexpected job loss, breakdown of a relationship and the failure to be chosen for an important dance role or theater part. Conflict and pain have brought us closer together as a shared common experience in our own group. It's part of what has defined us as a family."**

her. Our family's sense of humor comes in handy, as my mom can find the humor in everything!"

Still another person reflects: "My husband and I have had various struggles because we had children later in life and had older parents at the same time, and all the crises related to those two generational ends. It was a struggle to make the marriage work, but we worked hard to blend our differences. Another difficult struggle for me was trying to help my parents in the final few years of their life. A close friend, who was like a sister to me, and I both lost our parents over the same four years, one parent in each consecutive year. I have never endured such difficulty."

For sure, many tough questions crop up when struggle pounds at our family hearth. Some struggles act like night thunder rumbling the house walls, others like streaks of lightening scorching the ground, and others like "be careful" warnings to rush and cuddle inside. At what point does struggle stop making its members stronger and weaken them? How does a family identify this switch and seek outside help? Are there particular struggles, such as alcoholism, that are always destructive? And how does a family react to struggle with tolerance and love without getting ripped apart in the process? Let's explore, as best we can, these difficult topics.

Struggle Can Be Episodic or Enduring

Struggle can be a single event or an ongoing saga. It involves pain, conflict and, hopefully, breakthrough and resolution. Witnessing this mother's intense struggle will give you a feeling for the deep anguish that she has experienced over many years: "I grew up in a family that I would say had no soul, no connectedness, no support, no unity, no acceptance, and no authenticity, trust, or commitment. Therefore there was no happiness, no joy, no peace, no compassion, and no harmony. I always vowed that if I ever had my own family it would *not* be like the one I had growing up." She adds: "I think I always had some kind of innate sense of self, of who I was and who I wanted to be—and even more so, who I didn't want to be—and, for the most part, for the first twenty years or so of our marriage, *our* family was the opposite of the one I grew up with. I think if family members stay connected, united and supportive, the soul of the family can overcome any struggles." Continuing, she shares her experience witnessing addiction wear at the family soul: "when a member of the family loses their own 'soul' through addiction, it affects every other member and each member deals with it in their own individual way. They may take on the role of the persecutor, the enabler, the 'good' kid, the rescuer, or the victim. When someone succumbs to addiction, not only do they disconnect from their own 'self,' but they also sever relationships with those they are closest to. The addiction becomes the only important thing in their life. There is nothing more heartbreaking to the other family members than watching the addict's 'light' go out, as they spiral downward."

> **"There is nothing more heartbreaking to the other family members than watching the addict's 'light' go out, as they spiral downward."**

Sometimes Struggle Ends in Detached Love

Searching, engaged and hopeful, she continues. "This is the struggle our family is facing now, and this was also the struggle my childhood family faced. However, in my childhood family the addictions were present from the very beginning of the family so there was no foundation on which to even build a family soul; basic survival became the priority, and fear was what my siblings and I faced every day." She adds: "The addictive parent lost their 'heart and soul' and the other parent played the role of the enabler. There was great poverty, but I don't think that destroys the soul of the family, I think beyond losing your own soul, what really destroys the soul of the family is fear and anger." Poignantly she continued: "My current family did have a good foundation but it is still in danger of losing its 'soul' because the addiction is ongoing and the rest of our family has not stayed connected and has not pulled back together in unity. In the beginning, we all did pull together with support, to get help for our child, but it has become more and more apparent that this family member does not want it." From a depth of life wisdom, she concluded: "Addictive disease only gets better when the addict wants it to get better, regardless of how much the family longs for changes. Our family could only be united and connected again if we were all able to detach with love from the family member who has the disease of addiction, and hope that some day they would come back to us."

Weary from worrying about her family members, this mother said she tries to replace her anxiety with positive thoughts and actions. "Not always, but I'm working on it." Reflecting on the impact, she observed: "Our family has spent too much time in the last five years focused on our child's addiction and recovery. Our marriage has been bruised and battered from years of neglect, and our family is disconnected. My spouse and I have dealt differently with this family issue and unfortunately we are not on the same page with how we are addressing it." Observing transparently, she revealed: "Dealing with a family issue of this magnitude changes us all, and we have found ourselves thinking, saying and doing things that are completely out of character, out of a desperation to save our loved one. Anger, grief and resentment all create road blocks." Concluding intimately: "In the end, we each have to focus on saving our individual selves, to go towards love, not fear. Sometimes the only thing left to do is to surrender and accept that which you cannot change or control."

Other Struggles End in Joyful Resolution

Another family shared their biggest struggle and their "family work" to overcome it. They all took part in getting a fellow member to see a therapist. It was a group problem and it took group effort to help the individual. She had lost her job, was in a bad relationship, had been making risky choices and was in debt. She needed help and yet she was frozen by inaction. Her sister helped to get her evaluated by a therapist. The findings revealed she was bipolar and needed therapy. The same sister tracked down a treatment in cognitive therapy, which proved to be very helpful. After the daughter realized that she needed the therapy, she started to make progress. It took time, but without her supportive family desperately trying to make it happen, the soul of their family would still be struggling.

Remembering her state of devastation prior to seeking therapy, the daughter said: "I feel that I was a struggle for my whole family and caused a lot of conflict and pain. My family rallied around me and saved me." Her mother admits: "Everyone, including the son-in-laws, were supportive and helpful. She could not have done this by herself; she would have gotten so low that she would have ended up in some sort of institution. In the beginning she resisted a lot of their help." The daughter insisted at the time: "I don't need this, you are wrong. Leave me alone, I know what I am doing." Consequently, they all ended up in counseling. And the mother said that being a part of the family therapy circle was critical to healing the family bond. "We all needed a little help in our family dynamics. Cognitive therapy worked her miracle and her therapist was remarkable. Personally, I think we all could use some therapy regularly. It is so very helpful to have guidance with our problems."

Success with resolving problems on the family front requires communication, self-awareness and personal effort. In her conclusion, the mother mused: "We try to deal with a problem as best we can, when it happens. It makes our bond stronger. When we ignore things or try to pretend they don't happen, it makes things worse. Communication plays a key role. We are a very close family. It still takes a lot of work to do the communicating and be aware of each other."

Another parent shared her strategies to work through struggle with her two sons during their teen years. I think this situation and example is applicable to all peoples' struggles. "You just have to keep responding and moving forward, and hopefully each step is a move towards progress. You have to know that your children each have a family tool kit that says, 'we are not going to stop loving you, we are not going to judge you, and we are going to support you.' We have always said to our kids, 'we are not looking for a super achiever, just your best effort, something you care about, and that is what matters to us.'"

Unresolved Struggle Eats Away at Family Soul

Strife and struggle is often present in a family's patterns of interaction. Let me share three conflicts among three different families. The first conflict was a volatile relationship between a father and younger daughter, who both liked to take control of family situations. Almost every time they were together, the family dynamics ended in fury with the father walking away from his daughter, who was tearfully trying to explain her feelings. The mother would step in trying to mediate both sides, tempers would grow heated, out of control and divisive. They *all* had a difficult time bridging their relationships and the family bond was slowly weakened.

The next two conflicts seem uneventful, but let me assure you, each was enormously painful and corrupted the family dynamics in its own way. The first involved a husband who constantly watched television, turning it on when he walked in the door, and expressing no interest in family interactions, like playing sports, or a board game, or even sitting down for the family meal. The second was a spouse's dangerous car driving style. He had anger issues as soon as he got in the car. Everyone became his enemy—bikers, pedestrians and other cars. Additionally, his driving habits included texting and emailing. Both matters created major obstacles to healthy family interactions, and made it difficult to rise above the issues in order to reach a higher level of family connection and communication. Unresolved conflicts such as these split the family apart. An inability to settle differences makes it difficult to be in family soul synchronicity and enjoy a sense of love and togetherness.

Struggle Can Provide Insight

Lastly, young children themselves experience struggle. Witness a fifth grade child's perspective on the difficulties he had when his grandfather reached the point of needing hospice care, after living with lymphoma for ten years. His mother decided to move to be with her sick father for four months and took along his younger brother. He shared his challenges and struggles from this experience: "Last March my mother and younger brother flew out to stay with my grandparents. Grandfather had been sick with cancer and he was getting worse. I chose to stay home because it was an important time for me, being the last year in my old elementary school and a lot was happening in my life." However, he stresses: "There was one major problem. My dad's commute to work was over an hour long. To make things easier, dad usually spent most of the week at the work location. The only solution for me was to stay at friend's houses on the nights dad was not home. This meant that I had to manage having a change of clothes, living in multiple places, doing my homework, and being very self-reliant." He reflected with a certain amount of reserved pride: "I learned a lot from this experience. I observed how other families lived in comparison to my own. Many times the families were very different. I think most importantly though I had to become independent. I realized the importance of family. I also learned a little bit of what it was like with only one parent. While at friends houses, I practiced how to act in another person's home. There is a saying, 'if it doesn't kill you, it makes you stronger.' At moments, I felt this way about my challenging experiences."

For four months this young boy single handedly managed his situation. He had to get up in the morning, remember his schoolwork, saxophone and hockey skates. He knew his mom was not going to be away forever and said to himself, "I can do this." This challenging experience brought learning and struggle to each family member as they coped with the stress of caring for their aging family member, and yet the gift of this struggle was a stronger, more loving connection to the soul of the family.

As these multiple family situations exemplify, struggle is an inherent quality in the creation or destruction of the family heart and soul. Just as family members feel close when they celebrate an important event or accomplishment, they can also experience togetherness when they are going through hard times. Struggling through the trenches with someone you love can make you feel even closer. Struggle has the power to deepen the family bond and profoundly connect the group.

Finding the Silver Linings in Struggle and Change

Let's move to the topic of change. The soul of the family evolves over time when family members do things together that nourish both their individual and collective spirits. Two parents shed light here. The first, who grew up in a family with a parent and siblings with alcoholism, had this to disclose: "Growth as individuals affects not only each person, but the family too. When family members grow individually, the soul of the family does also, as long as there is still connection, support, unity, authenticity, commitment and trust among family members." When these requirements don't exist, it is not easy to work through struggle and change. And sometimes you cut the cord, reflected one father of three adult children. "The soul of the family is all about connecting, but you have to choose who to connect with and then you have to care for those connections. And over time you have to discard some connections, change others, and reinforce and encourage additional ones. It is a massive life-long process."

The family soul is in constant change. It evolves through five developmental periods from birth through death (i.e. childhood, teen years, young adult, adult and elderly). Different caretakers step in to care for everyone in the family circle. The six soul experiences appear at different points in time, in no particular order. Think of humor, emotion, acceptance, renewal, togetherness and struggle all tossed into the same pot and you get the idea—rampant change. New family members join. Friends and special people are invited in. Each connection, whether old or new, reshapes the group and must be maintained and nurtured. Children and parents get new obligations, some move to different locations, experiences are shared, relationships change, and the family expands and grows. The old pair of shoes comes to mind again. These shoes have stretched and expanded, and hopefully still fit with time and age. They may be weather-beaten, worn, and slip off—but we still choose them as our favorites.

Making and Caring for Connections

One older father who I interviewed summarized this changing process rather cogently. "My family consists of a continuous connection process that creates the soul of the family. Taking care of the soul means deepening, strengthening, reinforcing and re-energizing our connections and bonds. We must find ways to connect with new individuals too. Often I use my intuition. I just know intuitively that I need to connect with another soul. For me, connecting with other people constitutes a big part of what I do. Multiple connections with others of all ages: older when we were younger, and younger when we are now older." Continuing, he clarifies and shares more detail: "Once you connect with others, there is a reciprocating connection and a mutual energy…this is why it is ever changing." We live in the midst of a continuous process of encountering change and welcoming new connections that reshape the soul of the family.

Struggle can strengthen or weaken a family soul. It exists everywhere and comes in many forms. It can be episodic or enduring. Sometimes struggle ends in detached love—or it ends in joyful resolution. Almost always, struggle can provide insight. Unresolved struggle eats away at the soul of the family.
Find the silver linings in struggle and change.

Tool #9: See the Change

To absorb the idea of constant change and the need to care for each connection, it may be helpful to "see" it. Take out a sheet of paper. On the top, write down the following headings: five family stages, caretaker and "my" family members. At each family stage, different family members may initiate humor, communicate emotion, offer acceptance, facilitate renewal, create togetherness, or cause struggle.

Five Stages	Caretaker	Members Defined
Childhood/1		
Teen/2		
Young Adult/3		
Adult/4		
Elderly/5		

Now, think about each of these stages, as they relate to your family and its unique composition. Ask yourself, who the caretaker is and was at each stage. Who has been included within your traditional family group? What unique mix of friends, pets and special people has been invited in to join your family? Now, realize that all of these influences—family stage, caretaker and membership composition—are in a constant state of interaction and flux.

Constant Change From Six Soul Experiences

Along with evolving family stage, caretaker and member mix, there is a shift in the expression of humor, emotion, acceptance, renewal, togetherness and struggle. Each of these soul experiences can also bring pervasive change. The family soul adjusts and transforms to accommodate this change. For example, the family soul may have constant struggle and very little humor when an alcoholic is on a drinking binge. In an extremely difficult situation like this one, when a family member is in trouble, all six experiences would serve as positive influences, as they could re-fuel the depleted group. Yet, during this complicated period, laughter or humor may be non-existent. There is emotional rejection, little acceptance, no renewal or revitalizing energy, forced togetherness and pervasive struggle.

The opposite scenario occurs when life is going very well—really clicking—and exciting events are exploding off the map. Then the six soul experiences are expressed in abundance. There is lots of humor, high emotion, considerable acceptance, revitalizing energy, a tight feeling of togetherness and relatively little struggle. A dramatic shift comes about as though the light is now turned on.

One Family's Continual Change

The tenor and tone of the family soul *also* changes with life's challenges and situations. It can be buoyed by good news and evolve to be healthy and strong. Or it can succumb to disintegration and despair with tragedy and misfortune. One insightful parent shares her personal family story in which a succession of changing family origins, traditions, a tragic death, and remarriage immeasurably shaped their family. "I grew up in a family of nine children. My mother was born in Ireland, worked as a nurse in England and came to New York on her own (the only one in her family to do so). She met my dad, a devout Catholic, Marine and businessman. Religion was extremely important in our family and I think Sunday mornings were always the time where we all went to church together and had our special Sunday breakfast and took our Sunday drives. It was a time where we all were together and connected."

She continues: "My mother was diagnosed with breast cancer when my youngest sister was seven years old and she died three years later. Although our faith got us through the grief, I think we lost the soul of the family when my mother died. My father just moved on as if nothing had changed, but many of us felt lost and disconnected, especially when my dad married a woman he had know for six months within a year of my mother's death." She notes: "His new wife was different in every way. My mother with her strong Irish brogue was petite and beautiful, demure, but strong and an amazing mother. This new mom was tall and heavy, confrontational, critical, and three of her five children were estranged from her." Continuing, "Since I was the second eldest and working in Chicago, I became the 'mother' to my younger brothers and sisters. My father seemed to abandon us as soon as he married, burying himself in work and golf."

The conflict and struggle worsened: "I struggled to keep intact all the things that had defined our family and seemed to be at constant odds with the new wife, to the point where I was no longer allowed in my family home even for holidays. I still stayed in constant contact with my younger siblings and took up battles with my father when it was appropriate (i.e. my parents always insisted that we all get a college education, whereas the new wife felt two years of community college was enough and convinced my father *not* to pay for college educations anymore). My other sisters and I funneled money and care directly to the younger ones in our family."

The older siblings connected together around a mutual goal, to ensure that the spirit and soul of their mom lived on in her children who were still living at home. Once the youngest member was finally out of the house and in college, they felt they had accomplished everything they could do. The nine children became incredibly bonded to each other and still are. Although they were all disappointed that their father allowed his children to be treated in this way, they realized that he did it out of ignorance. To him, the wife takes care of the kids and the house, while his duties were to work. He didn't know how to rectify the hole that the loss of their mother created.

Concluding, she said: "My dad is one of the kindest, sweetest, fun-loving men. He was always the organizer of the block-wide softball games; kick the can or basketball tournaments. Other kids in the neighborhood would ring the doorbell and ask if my dad was coming out to play today." Today, her dad is very much a part of his children and grandchildren's lives. They adore him and have accepted his wife.

This person believed that the soul of her family existed more with the nine children because they all lived through their hardship together and have great admiration for each other. She said that her youngest brother and sister are like her children, even though the age difference is eleven and thirteen years. She says she still cries when they bring up stories of what they had to go through; she said she feels like she somehow let them down, but they never see it that way.

Now, shift to her nuclear family—and a different family stage. The difference in how she has brought up her own family was intentional and directed by her past experience. She knew she wanted a more vocally supportive and accepting family than the one she was raised in. Her exceptionally strict father was never someone to test out new ideas on, especially not ideas that varied from his own. Together with her husband, she sought to know their two daughters more personally and to have them learn to easily express themselves and their ideas. When they were very young, they put on music and danced around the room. They supported their efforts at trying music, sports, dance, languages and making friendships. They hosted their children's friends for play dates, coached their teams and adjusted their careers to be available as parents. They tried to convey their love and the knowledge that they supported their children whether their team won or lost, or whether or not they were picked for chorus. They grounded their children in religion to challenge them with the possibility of things greater than their own understanding.

As their children grew and became increasingly independent, there were ups and downs. Their children tested them, but as parents they found their spines. They tried to not get bogged down in the petty arguments that adolescents love to generate. All along, they preserved their times of family closeness with trips to the beach, shared holiday traditions and just being there to convey love and support.

Now, their "children" are twenty-four and twenty-seven years old. As adults, they are comfortable expressing their ideas. They continue to mature and face new challenges daily, and their actions indicate their evolving confidence. As a family, they have a closeness that only a fully adult family can achieve. The conversations are more direct, the issues are more advanced and challenging and their willingness to engage with their parents is more obvious. The adult children can share ideas and concerns in confidence and their parents learn from them.

❧ ❧

Whether long ago or in the present, transformation and challenge are a constant realty. The influence of the family's caretaker, members and soul experiences are pervasive and ever-changing. Be open to these shifts in the family dynamic and learn to grow with them.

Tool #10: Be Forgiving

An astute grandmother who described herself as her family's caretaker reflected from a depth of life wisdom, "I have learned that one of the greatest gifts I can give to my family is to let go—cease wanting, expecting, judging. Letting go and forgiveness are the same to me. The forgiveness of myself and others leads to a more joyful family soul."

Know that the soul is at work when we forgive. Forgiveness helps us shed negative emotions and energy in order to heal. Forgiveness brings transparency and emotional clarity. One can then shift and focus on the more positive things in family life. I think the work of forgiveness acts like cleansing rain. Just like heavy spring rains cleanse the earth and freshen the air, forgiveness too is a powerful purifier for the family.

Forgiveness Enables A Family To Begin Anew

One family experienced a remarkable catharsis when a difficult issue was at last put to rest, affording them all a new beginning. While they all had struggled, they now had reached a point of understanding and resolution. Let me explain.

After several painful and difficult years, shared one father, a son telephoned from college to individually ask each family member, parents and younger siblings alike, if they would forgive him for his behavior during this time. He vividly recalled many of the trying incidents, reminding them all of the details of his difficult past. While the family members individually told him that they forgave him, he reassuringly asked each of them a second time, as though to permanently reassert the fact in his mind. They *all* felt cleansed.

The soul is at work when there is forgiveness. The rains of forgiveness poured down again on another family's situation, as shared by a wife. A business partner criticized her husband, for several years creating tension in his professional life. Her husband had not forgiven the business associate, nor had he forgiven his own parents for some things that occurred long ago while growing up. To prepare his heart for forgiveness he realized, finally, that to harbor past negative memories and grudges held him back. It was this revelation that inspired his change of heart. Whamo. He forgave them all. Finally liberated from negative emotions, he too was liberated. His time and energy were available to him for positive events and interactions. For years, negative feelings consumed an incredibly large amount of time. Letting go of these allowed for a purification to occur. A shedding and freeing occurred on the business *and* home front where he grew up. Clarity and strength were available to him now, as he too was cleansed by forgiving others. His soul did a little dance!

> **To wait for the person who has caused the damage to forgive could consume a lifetime, like puffy clouds speeding by without letting loose their rain.**

Just as the spring solstice is a new beginning, forgiving family members, a friend, or colleague opens the door to positive energy and intention. It gives the one who forgives a sense of peace. To wait for the person who has caused the damage to forgive could consume a lifetime, like puffy clouds speeding by without ever letting loose their rain. Forgive now and experience a sense of peace and delight in the present. Ask yourself: Have I experienced the joy of being forgiven? Have I recently been the forgiver? If you can answer "yes," then forgiveness has indeed cleansed you.

The Power of Humility

Forgiveness is an act of humility. Allowing humility to permeate your everyday activities will produce a remarkable result: Not only will you feel more balanced and self-assured, but people will feel more relaxed and confident approaching you and will be more excited to be with you. Abide by the following eight guidelines for just a week, and you will notice a change. Discover the power of humility—do these simple action steps.

1. Express concern for the problem at hand.

2. Take responsibility for your failures and learn from them.

3. Express gratitude for the good and bad—both are blessings!

4. Admit mistakes.

5. Apologize when you are wrong.

6. Give credit to others for their help in your success.

7. Show patience and forgiveness when treatment is unfair.

8. Be gracious when accepting feedback.

A deeply connected family centers on weaving humility into daily interactions. If there is a prima donna in the family group, this person can upset the family equilibrium. Importantly, people who embrace humility *nurture* the energy of those around them. But with humility, families make an effort to listen to others and accept their individuality. They express concern for others, show gratitude, admit mistakes, apologize when wrong, give credit to others, demonstrate patience and forgiveness and graciously accept feedback. They take responsibility for their own failures and learn from them. They create a healthy, caring energy. When acts of humility permeate the group, the family bond strengthens and deepens.

Ten Ways to Reconcile Deep Wounds

When the wounds are deep and the hurt has been going on for a long time, just saying, "I am sorry" may not be sufficient. First, recognize what caused the rift or problem. Maybe your adult son or daughter crossed the line, or maybe you did. In either case, it was terribly wounding albeit it never was intended to be so. To make matters more intense, your older child's explosive behavior might indicate some type of physical or mental illness, especially if there is unexplainable acting out. Or other wounds might be intentional, as in the case of an in-law clandestinely "stealing" one's son away, a problem shared by one interviewee. Other times, you can't figure out what went wrong and, over time, it just seems to get messier and more problematic.

So what can you do during these extremely challenging family times? Take it slowly. Try these ten ways to expand your repertoire of choices to reconcile the deep wounds, as developed from my interviews, psychological research and personal experience.

1. **Get rid of self-righteousness.** Stop framing the situation in terms of "who's right and who's wrong."

2. **Instead of denying feelings, put them into words.** "You must feel really upset and embarrassed about what happened at the party. I am slowly seeing what a mess I made for you by my actions. I drank too much and should not have put the moves on your boss. It was stupid of me."

3. **Actively listen!** Often we simply fail to listen *carefully* to what another person is telling us. Focus on deeply and selflessly understanding your family member's point of view.

4. **Use *lots* of humility.** Be willing to admit that it was your mistake and perhaps a stupid one at that! We *all* make mistakes, but we all don't admit that we do. Model how to be humble on the family front. Families should talk about problems and be bluntly honest about their own thoughts and feelings. Get them out.

5. **Put "I'm sorry" in writing.** A letter may work better than verbal conversation, especially if the problem is a serious or deep one. Words on paper can be read over and over so your apology can be absorbed.

6. **Brainstorm to come up with an action plan.** "Let's try to come up with some ideas as a family for how to prevent this from happening again." List all ideas and possible solutions without evaluating to rectify the situation or problem.

7. **Step back!** Your adult child or family member may not be ready to resolve the issue. Trust that time will work for you. Waiting to resolve the problem may be the very best tactic. Avoid stepping in until the time is right and positive action steps can be more effective. Retreat does not mean you are giving up; rather, you are looking for that opportune moment to positively engage and make peace.

8. **Get some outside help.** Ask another family member, friend or counselor to intervene and shed some light on the rift or problem. Realize, however, that this may cause your enraged family member to roar with anger, but in some cases an "outsider" can be an effective peacemaker.

9. **Hang in there.** Keep trying. It may take a lot more conversations and letters to turn around the situation. Don't give up. Days or months or perhaps years may resolve the rift. Maybe an unexpected twist will work to your advantage. We all become more forgiving with time and age.

10. **Put it on the back burner!** If there is no resolution in sight, give yourself permission to focus on yourself. Enjoy life! Take time to smell the peonies in your back yard or take a trip with your closest friend.

Know that the soul is at work when there is forgiveness. Forgiving family members, a friend, or colleague opens the door to positive energy and intention. Allow humility to permeate your everyday activities—and it will produce a remarkable result too.

18. Celebrate the Harvest

"As we see it, our sons are growing up to be humble, hard-working, thoughtful, well-rounded human beings and we are, in turn, learning from them. 'The fruits' are perhaps that our sons love each other, get on very well together and support each other. They each have a high emotional quotient, which we feel is an endearing quality for three individual brothers to have. We believe that these qualities have probably come about through a combination of both nature and nurture and instilling values in their daily lives."

—Interviewed parent

The harvest is a time of bounty. It is the process of gathering mature crops from the fields. Additionally, the harvest marks the end of the growing season for a particular crop. It is also a time of seasonal celebration. Families too reach a time of harvest. Members possess kindness and generosity. They feel a sense of friendship. They have learned to express the qualities of gratitude, compassion, humility, service, and most of all, deep love and happiness—the cornucopia. It is a time to dance and celebrate.

What are the "fruits" that come from spending time together? Connected hearts share a harvest. These are the positive outcomes, small or large, of shared time. How do these positive outcomes take place within the family dynamic? Let's listen in on how some families have reaped their fruit.

Parents Weighing In On "Outcomes"

Talking about their harvest, one parent explained: "I think service, generosity and compassion have come from the time our family has spent together. I see these qualities in all of us. This has been fostered by helping each other and by reaching out to others as well. Every year we would either adopt a family or collect letters from children in need and we all participated in buying, wrapping and sending gifts, even sometimes meeting with the recipients. Even little day-to-day things have fostered these qualities, like helping a friend or family member in need."

Another person believes that her family values were established long before she was born. "I believe the foundation was laid by my ancestors and carried forward to today. Our morals and values were being shaped even before we could speak our first words. We were taught a Southern hospitality, to respect one another, be kind to elders, say, 'yes mam, and yes sir'. We weren't raised in a home of hollering and screaming or cursing and swearing. It was honor your mother and your father." She continues: "My mother speaks highly of her father, and what a kind and quiet spirit he had been until he died when she and her brother were kids. My mother said when her dad died, my grandmother sat her and her brother down at the table and told them, 'we don't have much, but we will always be there for one another. We will get through this together, as a family.'" She stressed: "She taught her children the same scripture she was taught, which was from Proverbs 22:6, 'Train a child in the way he should go, and when he is old, he will not depart from it.' This is not to say that we've always done the right thing, or made the right decisions, but somehow we've been able to come back to what we know in our hearts is right."

Reflecting on the positive outcomes in their children, another parent shared: "Now that our children are grown, we have just as much fun with them as we did when they were little, and fun is important. It is rather amazing to see what fine, caring people they have become, with the courage of their convictions, but accepting of others' views. I think part of how this came about was that we all have always wanted to see and do the right thing, whatever that is, before our own personal desires."

> **"This is not to say that we've always done the right thing, or made the right decisions, but somehow we've been able to come back to what we know in our hearts is right."**

More Fruits

As to their family "fruits," one mother shared her ideas. "We have always opened our hearts to others. We share stories with others as they share them with us. We always try to include those who don't have a "permanent" home. We've had many international relationships in the U.S. and abroad and these connections have brought great friendship and learning to both sides of those relationships." When asked how this come about? she said: "People in our families were raised to be kind and helpful, plus they were just genuinely interested in others. It wasn't something that had to be done or for which we would be acknowledged, we just acted that way or reached out. Life is a two-way street; when you do something nice, you get a reward back."

Two parents shared some precious evidence of the positive outcomes. The first parent noted: "I have to mentally separate the unexpected willingness of a recalcitrant adult child to unload a dishwasher without being asked, from the feeling I get as a mother when my two children want to 'be' with me, want me to know and spend time with their friends, want my presence at a time when I might expect they would prefer to be alone." She continues: "These warm my heart, and makes me feel we are a 'unit'. An unexpected act of kindness is absolutely welcome, but, if I think of 'soul,' it's the bigger 'it' that comes from the acceptance I feel from our now adult children. It was when my twenty-two-year-old unexpectedly wrote his 'credits' as the lead on his final school play to 'his amazingly supportive parents'. Or, asked me to accompany him for support when he had his professional headshots taken. I didn't expect it at all, tried to stay out of the way, but it felt like equality and acceptance." And those are delicious fruits, I might add.

The second parent shared what her son wrote when he applied to middle school. It too showed the fruits of their togetherness. It is a child's perspective on the soul of his family. His admission's essay included this brief excerpt: "My mom is a creative and kind person. She is big on recycling, not wasting food, thank-you notes, etc. and does a lot of volunteer work. My dad works as chief financial officer at a school. Although we are not very athletic, dad is the one who taught us about sports and he has a million different sayings about every topic, most of them came from his dad. ('A penny saved is a dollar earned.')" He continues: "My brother is a kid who has many different interests – palm trees, coconuts, Egypt, creepy crawlers, and now he is into cars." This is not the ordinary list of preferences here such as T.V. shows, digital games, etc. One gets the strong sense that there are lots of positive outcomes from this family's togetherness—with many fruits for future harvest.

Continuing, their other son was asked this question when he applied to middle school: "If you could be *invisible* for a day, what would you do?" His reply: "I would go into the blue hills and I would watch the animals, and get up close to the deer, and see the bunnies." Rather than sneak in a movie theater or a locker room (while invisible), or hang out in a mall with other tween companions, he chose to hang out in nature, illustrative of a strong positive influence from his family.

Fruits for the Family and the Marriage

There are fruits for the family itself—and the benefits are enormous. Family time together solidifies the bond, uplifts the spirit, and allows for the growth of family members. Shares one mother: "We love getting together. We anticipate it, enjoy it; our home is a place where intense growth discussions have taken place, where neighbors have rallied and joined in and contributed love and support. Where tree forts were built, trees planted, puzzles solved and all the time, the restorative salve of being together is smoothed over the fragile family soul, strengthening and supporting it, filling

> "Our home is a place where intense growth discussions have taken place, where neighbors have rallied and joined in and contributed love and support. Where tree forts were built, trees planted, puzzles solved and all the time, the restorative salve of being together is smoothed over the fragile family soul, strengthening and supporting it, filling in the gaps with humor glue and physical hugs and strenuous walks with the playful dogs that are special."

in the gaps with humor glue and physical hugs and strenuous walks with the playful dogs that are special."

And finally, there are fruits for marriages too. A mother of an autistic son describes her harvest. Not only did their marriage endure the difficult times, they also reached a happy endpoint bearing fruit for both their transformed son and themselves as a refocused couple. She shares: "The soul of our family was possible because my husband and I were committed to our marriage, which managed to endure despite incredible stress. Our son could go weeks without sleeping a night. We were zombies. But we did not have a choice; we had another son to nurture. We kept each other going, and we always celebrated those small moments when we could be adults and finish a sentence." And their contented endpoint: "Now that our children are more or less out of the house, we enjoy being together and adults again. We have music and fires and wine and conversations and quiet and freedom. None of that would be possible if our adult son were not living in a program that is absolutely perfect for him. He has made strides we never imagined possible. His behavior is calm and happy. He is transformed. So long as the soul of our family is happy, we are, too."

Appreciation of Each Other Grows

Sometimes the fruit is when family members see each other's strengths and accomplishments more clearly—the illumination or knowledge of what makes each family member a star in their own right, often different and unique. "Our sense of admiration for each other and who we are and what we can do together is heightened," says one parent, adding, "I definitely know that each one of us is very charitable and giving and it makes us very happy to give back in some way." These are fruits for the picking.

Like the ripened apple at the end of the season, another interviewee says that appreciation of each other grows and deepens over time. She details: "I know I have a special bond with my sisters and that knowledge and companionship makes me happy and keeps me going through hard times. Another benefit is that you acknowledge and cultivate the bond, making the necessary time to nurture the relationship, and thus carry on and deepen the soul."

Time investment and involvement are commensurate with outcomes. Listen to this same person share her result from spending time together: "My sisters and I turn to each other as support through hard times and just through life in general. We have always relied on each other heavily while growing up and this has reached over now into our adult lives. We could always count on each other to commiserate, empathize, support and just be there for each other. It was this reliance and trust that has born the fruit of our relationship."

Similarly, there are more "fruits" to their relationship: "My sisters are my confidants and the people I go to for advice on just about anything. They have been there, looking over my shoulder, my entire life and have really shaped who I am today. I turn to them for just about everything, but they play different roles. My oldest sister I turn to for general life advice, and I see her more as a parental role. She speaks and I listen. My middle sister I see as a peer, and we chat back and forth about personal problems and things I am pondering. They are both very sweet, loving, responsible and always looking out for me. I feel they care about me in a truly deep way that I take comfort in."

Pickle Harvest

My mom had a pickle harvest every late summer and early fall. She started making pickles when she was twenty-eight years old and continued well into her late nineties. Each year she easily made 150 to 200 quarts. In well over seventy years of pickle making, we figure she canned and distributed over ten thousand quarts to her friends and family. Her pickle harvest was something to dance and celebrate about indeed. To this day, I have friends tell me how much they miss her delightful and generous supply of dill, sweet, and bread and butter pickles. She stopped making them when she turned 97.

The word about her pickles got out. Friends from Chicago who couldn't make it to her 100th birthday party in Oregon, sent 120 pickle pens, along with several very large mason jars. The centerpiece at each table was a smaller mason jar filled with life size real-looking pickles (more of these pickle pens) stuffed inside. It was a telling sight. Guests were asked to write on note cards, using the pickle pens, and put their thoughts into the mason jars. All the guests knew that pickle production was a huge part of my mom's life.

I frequently had run-ins with her pickle preparation harvest. Once when I came back to visit my mom with my own young children, I recall getting up around midnight and going into the kitchen to witness my mom stabbing each cucumber three times with a large needle. She was standing next to a very large vat-like sweet pickle crock where the pickles would then sit for 20 days in a solution of vinegar, pickling spice, salt and sugar. This "stabbing" was essential so that the cucumbers absorbed the sugar and didn't shrink. I was invited into this step of the process, at this hour, as though we were playing a game of late-night cards!

> **I was invited into this step of the process, at this hour, as though we were playing a game of late-night cards!**

The daughter-in-law of one of my mom's best friends said hello to me at her birthday party. To my surprise, she said that she makes my mom's pickles every year, using the same trusted recipe. Curious how I connect pickles to family harvest or outcomes? Pickles are meticulously "put up" and shared, the recipe passed forward, and the harvest becomes bountiful. So it is with families. Cucumbers are to pickles, as small loving gifts are to strengthening our connections. We are grateful for the shared times and appreciative of the enduring bond.

Acknowledge the gift of each other, express joy and appreciate the growth of each person in your family—and share individual accomplishments with all!

Epilogue—
Share A Happy Life

As I was completing this book, I bumped into the words that I shared at my dad's funeral service. If you have stayed with me this far, I want to end on a personal note—one that I think captures the theme of becoming a happy family. As you can read, my dad had four values or "footprints" that ran through his life. They captured who he was—his life-focus. "Of all the places in the world, home was his favorite." He pursued happiness. It became a mindset. He lived a happy life. I wish the same for you. Discover your own footprints. They are unique to the world. Share them with each other. May you become—and celebrate—a happy family and give thanks for the time together.

Step-by-step Path

I have laid out a step-by-step path for bringing happiness home. One caring person with a happiness mindset can lead the crusade. Here are the pieces of the happiness puzzle:

- Identify and applaud your "caretaker"—the champion of the family soul;

- Recognize and apply practices that are integral to carving out happy and dynamic families: start a family of one's own, welcome in-laws and special people, bond with friends, discover a soul friend and add pets to the scene;

- Fortify the family soul with six vitamins or strengtheners—humor, emotion, acceptance, renewal, togetherness and struggle;

- Celebrate "the harvest"—appreciate the growth of each person in your family and share individual accomplishments with all; and

- Use the happiness tool kit—ten tangible ways to help families think and *do* differently: step back, seek balance and simplify, play often,

We hope this day will be a "Celebration of Life." The celebration of eighty-six and a half years together. If we can measure a life by the "footprints" it leaves, then Farmer Smith—"Papa"—left many footprints. But, there are **four** that run deep.

The **first** is his wonderful and long life with Bula—"Beah." They celebrated 57 years of marriage together last week in the hospital. His love for her was always strong, endearing, kind, gentle and forever. He simply adored every minute of the day with her.

A **second** footprint was the joy he had for his three children, Dean, Paul and Susan; their three spouses, JoAnn, Mary and Tom; and his ten grandchildren, Jeff, Ryan, Sara and Joe—John, James and Thomas—Jillian, Ellen and Lacey. His presence in their daily lives was strong and constant, whether cooking breakfast for us, driving us somewhere or waiting for us to return home. Of all the places in the world, HOME was his favorite. He was always there.

A **third** footprint was his love for the land—for hunting from it, growing on it, or connecting with it—whether it be his garden or down at his farm. He was a "farmer" at heart. He loved a newly cropped field, watching the grass seed grow and seeing fresh picked produce come down the conveyor belt.

A **fourth** footprint was his work, the care he took for what he did at the Stayton Canning Company, now Norpac Foods, and the growth, in turn, it experienced over the years. He deeply cared about those who he worked with, what they were building together and how they were going about it.

What we will miss most are those quiet times together. We each have our own special ones. Like reading the paper early in the morning, sitting outside on the patio at night, being together in the duck blind, and seeing "Papa" watch the faces of his grandchildren and smile at their expressions and activities. These moments brought him great happiness, as did the joy he brought to all of the lives who are here today.

Perhaps, if we can remember the **way** he said things, this will help us now.

"He is tougher than a boiled owl."

"That big frog—or—What are you little frogs doing?"

"Boys, we can't be late for the ducks."

"That felt good! I just hit the hell out of that golf ball. Where did it go?"

"Boys...it's time to get up for work."

"You're doing a good job, kid. Just stay at it."

May we celebrate his long and happy life. And give thanks for these wonderful years that we shared together.

speak from the heart, nurture equality and appreciate differences, praise descriptively, record memories, identify family values and rituals, listen selflessly and talk deeply, see the change and be forgiving.

Pursue happiness together and discover your family's soul along the way.

Interview Guide

1. How would you define the soul of the family?

2. What several words would you use to describe the soul of the family?

3. What does the soul of the family mean to you and how does your family "care" for it?

4. How does the soul of the family change and evolve over time?

5. Do you perceive the soul of the family to extend beyond immediate family members (i.e. grandparents, aunts, uncles, etc.) to include close friends?

6. How do you know if you have reached or experienced the soul of the family?

7. What are the values or key benefits of acknowledging the soul of the family?

8. Can you talk about your family's "struggle" (a single event or ongoing)? What role have struggle, search, conflict, pain and breakthrough played in your family?

9. Do you ever experience a family time when the energy is different, where you can actually feel the energy of love? Maybe rules disappear. Families have freer spirits. Members become "us" rather than "you" and "I." Can you describe this "spirit of us" energy and/or the joy of family love, and how it came about?

10. When is your family super happy together or "merry," how did you reach this peak place and what does this look/feel like? Conversely, what role does the "weary" play?

11. Family can be a safe place where members reach out embrace, comfort, applaud, cherish, awaken each other's powers and welcome everyone just the way they are—tears, fears, struggles, hardships and all. Do you agree? Why or why not? Can you add something here to further explain this point of view?

12. Can you talk about "the harvest"? Can you describe some of the "fruits" that are unique to your family? Have you every experienced these "fruits" to be a sense of service, generosity, friendship, kindness, equality, or compassion? How did these come about within your family dynamics?

13. Do you have a soul friend—a companion who is encouraging and helps you along your life path? If so, can you describe this person and how they help within your family?

14. What role do pets play in your family? Would you consider them to be part of your family's soul?

15. How does your family celebrate together, both small and large celebrations? How do you carve out quiet time together and what do you do?